DO THE THING,
HAVE THE POWER

OVERCOME SELF-DOUBT AND BUILD A
LIFE YOU LOVE

Hey Sarah,
Here's one with
a new cover.
Thanks for all
the support.

Chris

CHRIS BROCK

Cover design by Iro Ouranou

THANK YOU

This book is for my wonderful and extremely patient wife Victoria. I now know what joy is.

And it is also dedicated to my mother, father, brother and sister, who have supported me during my many adventures as I've tried to figure things out.

Thanks, too, to all my friends, colleagues, and every person I've ever met, who have all contributed to this thing called life and the filters through which I see it.

"Do the thing, and you will have the power."
– Ralph Waldo Emerson

Table of Contents

DO THE THING, HAVE THE POWER

PROLOGUE

THE TALE OF TWO WOLVES

An old man from the Lenape people of the Northeastern Woodlands was telling his grandson a story of two wolves. These wolves live inside each of us, engaged in a constant battle. One represents light and joy and hope, the other represents darkness, fear and sadness.

"Which wolf wins the fight?" Asked the little boy.

His grandfather replied: "The one you feed."

INTRODUCTION

"If you have no confidence in self, you are twice defeated in the race of life." – Marcus Garvey

I've lived a thousand different lives, been a thousand different people, in a thousand different places, and all along there was only one place I wanted to be. But the harder I tried, the further away it seemed to get. That place I wanted to be, the thing I desired the most, was success.

And I couldn't deal with it.

I've worked in a professional kitchen, in media, as a photographer, a van driver, a carer for the disabled, an emergency telephone operator, a kitchen hand, a journalist, a charity fundraiser, a podcaster and countless other things. Yet success always eluded me. I was waiting for my turn at life, my turn at the success I could see everyone around me enjoying. I was broke, unhappy, desperate. I didn't realise that the very act of waiting for success meant that it would always be beyond my reach.

As the years went by I fell victim to spells of depression, my confidence and self-esteem evaporated into air, and I lost all sense of my place in life. I felt that life was something that simply happened to me, and that I had no power over it. I had no influence over my own existence. All this waiting was hard work, and I was tired.

And then, slowly, it dawned on me. A growing realisation that everything I needed to be a success had been with me for my entire life. All these jobs I'd taken to keep a roof over my head and put food on my table, held the answer to reaching my dreams. Every experience I'd had, every job I'd done, every life I'd lived, every person I'd been and every person I'd met, all provided me with a piece of a jigsaw that put me in a unique position to reach that thing I'd been looking for all along. And ironically, all that I needed to do was let go.

From London to Indonesia, from the front seat of a van to a corner office in Manhattan, I had gained the answers I had been searching for, but I simply couldn't see it. I had no idea that my whole life I'd been gaining experiences and insights that could deliver everything I ever wanted if only I could open my eyes and acknowledge them. I had no idea that I was fully equipped to be the person I wanted to be, to live the life I wanted to live, and finally be able to 'deal with it'. All I had to do was recognise the power that I already had inside me – that we all have – but which is hard to see because it's hidden, buried beneath insecurities, or crushed by influences within us, and around us.

As soon as the penny dropped, like a baby learning to walk, I started taking small, tentative steps in the right direction. I began to understand that life was no longer something that just happened to me, but that I could gain a level of mastery over myself and my existence that would enable me to live life with grace and confidence, compassion, kindness and positivity, and not be intimidated by any circumstance, person or thing. I could move forward with positivity rather than constantly moving backwards with negativity. I could be the author of my own reality.

We all have the tools required to realise our goals, and when you recognise it and learn how powerful you really are, you can stop feeling insecure, stop feeling anxious, stop worrying what others think, and start getting on with the fine art of being the best version of yourself. You can start living the best version of your life, and share that positive energy with those around you and the wider world.

When you focus on wellness, on positivity, on ideas, on kindness and on action, there's nothing you can't achieve. When you understand the meaning of joy and gratitude, the sun will shine on your life like an endless summer. The only things stopping you are the baseless fears that serve no purpose other than to hold you back, the lies you tell yourself that choke you and stop you taking those first steps. It's time take back that power from the negative mindset that sabotages your best efforts, and start building the life you want.

Ralph Waldo Emerson famously said, "do the thing, and you will have the power." I struggled for a long time to understand what that meant, until one day the fog cleared and it hit me like a bolt of lightning. In these six simple words was the distillation of what it takes to be the best you can be, with the best life, with constant improvement. Another way of saying it is "take action, get the benefit".

How hard can that be? How much clearer does it need to be spelled out for us?

When you take action each day, as part of a unique daily practice that you'll build as you work through this book, you will develop a process of getting better, stronger, more powerful, and moving forward a little bit each day. And with these small steps you'll learn how to walk to a life that you can relish, enjoy and own for yourself.

We all have personal power, but for a lot of us it's so deeply buried we're completely unaware of it. At best we are taking actions that don't deliver any benefits, and at worst we are taking actions that take away our power and make our lives worse. We do things that are harmful to us, whether that means actions which are bad for our health or mental wellbeing, bad for our careers, or that simply keep us treading water, trapped in lives that appear to be going nowhere. We undermine ourselves with negative thinking that reinforces low self-esteem and lack of confidence; we engage in practices and behaviours that prevent us from reaching our goals; or we work hard day in day out, just to keep the roof over our heads, just to keep food on the table, the wolf from the door, without ever realising our full potential.

We give away our power to those who criticise us, tell us we aren't good enough, make us angry or insecure, or roll their eyes at our plans and reduce our capacity for achievement. We give away our power every time we use up our energy feeling sorry for ourselves, unsure of what to do next, worrying about what could go wrong. We give away our power every time we react automatically and let our negative emotions do the driving. But when you recognise the power that you already have, your skills and abilities, the positive aspects of your personality, your potential for greatness and your ability to improve yourself and your life, you'll want to hold on to it. You'll want to treasure it, nurture it. And you will begin to realise that this power will transform your life from something that merely happens to you into something that you can grasp, shape and make work for you. And when these transformations begin to happen, you'll start to wonder what else you're capable of.

I'm no scholar. I don't claim to be an expert in the human mind or a qualified psychologist. But I am an expert in my own life and I know what has helped me. This book is about my own journey, from being stuck and waiting for my turn (a turn that would never come), to taking ownership of my life and realising that it was always my turn from the very start. And I hope that by reading my story you will find the power that you already have within you and, like me, do what's needed to take your turn.

This book is about three simple steps:

1. Find your power.
2. Retain your power.
3. Grow your power.

When you understand that you already have the power, that the journey you've already been on is a part of your success story, and that the paradox of letting go of your dreams is vital to achieving them, you'll be well on the way to a new life.

You can get unstuck if you can recognise the tools that you already have at your disposal. You'll see that you already have the strength to turn your life around. You'll realise that you are the only one who can make it happen. And you'll see that the journey to a better life is, in itself, the better life.

We've all lived a thousand different lives, been a thousand different people in a thousand different places, struggling to understand just what it takes to get where we want to go and why our dreams have always eluded us. But simply turning up every day and doing the hard work, which is what we've always been told to do, isn't going to get us where we want to be tomorrow. The things that we've done to get where we are now will either keep us here, or slowly start to take us backwards. If we want to move forward in the direction we desire we need to take new, beneficial actions. We must master of the aspects of life that maintain our existence, and then start doing things – new things – that will move us beyond merely existing. We must gracefully master the ordinary in order to become extra-ordinary.

We must take actions that deliver benefits, small benefits at first, that get the wheels turning. We must take risks that, even if they don't work out at the time, will offer a benefit further down the line. As soon as we start to see how far we've come, it will provide the momentum to take us as far as we wish to go.

This book is about uncovering the things that make us

special, about taking ownership of our actions and our results, and about finding the power within us. It is about understanding that we have a unique set of attributes that separate us from the crowd, and can give us whatever we want. It is about living life on purpose and with grace, making decisions that will turn our lives into masterpieces that will elevate us from living the mundane to living the amazing.

This book is about the gradual art of graceful living, and living well. It's time to pick up the brush and start painting.

PART 1: FIND YOUR POWER

CHAPTER 1: LIFE SUCKS

"Life isn't about finding yourself. Life is about creating yourself."
– George Bernard Shaw

Life sucks. Other people have all the luck. It's not fair. He's better looking than me. She's got nicer hair than me. It's ok for them, they've got rich parents. They're just talented like that. He's cleverer than me, taller than me, doesn't have the problems that I have. He gets it. Why do bad things always happen to me? If that hadn't happened all those years ago, I wouldn't be in this terrible position. It's not my fault. It's their fault. It's her fault. It's his fault. It is my fault. It's all my fault. I'm just not very good. I'm not tall enough. I'm too short. I'm too fat. I'm too stupid. I'm too lazy. I'm too negative. I'm too white. I'm too black. I'm too blonde. I'm too tall. I'm too arrogant. I'm too ugly. I was born this way. I'll never achieve anything. I'm a failure. I'm unpopular. I'm not very likeable. I'm universally hated. I'm in a world that hates me. I'm in a Universe that won't let me succeed. I'm doomed to failure for the rest of my life. I wish I was dead. I hate myself. I deserve to fail. I deserve all the bad things that happen to me. I just don't get it.

Life sucks.

Ever have one of those thoughts pop into your head during a dark day? You might be in the shower, minding your own business, letting your mind wander, and suddenly you're thinking about how much you hate your body, or you're ashamed because you're not organised enough to fit exercise into your daily routine, or you feel like a failure because you can't afford a gym membership.

What about three of those thoughts during a difficult week? Perhaps you get out of bed and find that you're hating yourself because you didn't study harder at school, and now you must go to a job that reminds you that you're a lazy failure every day.

Ok, how about all those thoughts all the time? Every day. From the moment you wake up to the moment you try to go to sleep? Your head buzzing with reminders of things you've done to embarrass yourself, memories of all the times you've failed, reasons for not doing new things (usually because you'll fail, or just not make it to the end), times when you've let yourself down, or reasons to be ashamed of yourself. A constant stream of anxieties about money, about what people think of you, of how all those decisions you made were the wrong decisions, of how much of a slog life is that it takes all your effort just to get out of bed in the morning, when you'd rather not have to face life at all.

Because life sucks.

While everyone else seems to get all the good stuff, the rewards, the lives they've always wanted, you've been working hard for years, patiently waiting your turn, only for it to come to all those people around you, but never to you. Instead you just have a string of bad luck, of anti-climaxes, missed opportunities, terrible misfortune, and unhappiness. But, to be honest, that's probably what you deserve because you are, after all, a failure. You missed that day at school where everyone else was taught the secret to a happy, successful life, and now you exist in an infinite rut of gloom while everyone else is sucking the marrow out of their wonderful, blessed existences.

You inhabit a Universe that is tipped against you. Every day is a battle, and nothing ever goes your way. So why even bother? You're broke, in a job that you hate, and you hate yourself for all your obvious flaws and a whole load more. Why is life so unfair?

Well, I'm going to let you in to a secret. Something that will start to change the way you think about life and about yourself. This secret, that really isn't a secret at all, will start you on a journey that begins where you are right now, floundering, stuck, miserable and unable to 'deal with it', and it will lead you to own your life, to bend it to your will, to own it, to live it on purpose. You will understand what it means to master the fine art of living. You will take joy from the smallest things, and realise that the power to have the life you've always dreamed of has been with you all along – you've just had the wool pulled over your eyes.

When you begin to understand the power that you've got within you, that you've been denying all this time, you'll understand that anything is possible. And when you realise that life isn't something that just happens outside your will, that you are responsible for where you are now, and because of that you can be responsible for realising your full potential, you'll

23

understand there's magic all around you if you will only choose to look – and to move. You can do whatever you want, be whatever you want, once you understand the three words of that first simple secret:

LIFE JUST IS.

Life isn't unfair. But neither is it fair. Life just is. It can be ugly, and it can be beautiful, it can be gentle and it can be cruel. But it just is. It doesn't like, but neither does it hate. It just is, in the same way that a chair "just is". In the same way that a rock "just is", or a hill "just is". Life "just is".

This may go completely against what you're feeling right now. You may disagree with me entirely because from where you're sitting life seems pretty unfair. But that's exactly the point. All those attributes about life being cruel, or harsh, or beautiful, these are the meanings that you give to life from where you're sitting, from your perspective. These are reflections of the state you're in. When things don't go your way, you see life as unfair. When things do go your way, you see life as beautiful. But all along it's not life that's changing, it's you, and your perspective of life.

Life "just is" regardless of your situation, of your mood, or the rut you're in or the wave you're riding. Life just does its thing, always moving forward whether you like it or not, like a river following its course. And just like a river it can either bring sustenance to all the plants and animals that drink the clear, refreshing water at its bank, or it can bring destruction as it washes away anything that stands in its path. But just like a river, life has no agenda other than to go from the beginning to the end, and you can either dive in and swim, or you can stand there and drown. Either way, life will keep moving forward, and it's taking you with it, one way or another.

But if life isn't cruel, harsh or unfair, if it's just doing its thing regardless of what's happening to you, who's responsible for your circumstances? If life is not unfair, then what's to blame for things not working out in your favour when they appear to be working out in everybody else's favour?

All these things that have gone wrong for you along the way, that haven't worked out in your favour, that make you feel like you're drowning, that have led to you being where you are, in this place, in this state, and in this moment – they all have one thing in common. All those embarrassing moments you've had, those jobs you didn't get, the rejection letters you received, the debt you've accrued, the sleepless nights where you've been kept awake by guilt and regret, those times when you wished the earth would swallow you up, when you wished you'd never been born, or that you'd been born better, taller, faster, cleverer, to wealthier parents, a different race or in a different place – they all have one thing that connects them all.

And what's wonderful is that the same thing that connects all those terrible times, all that bad luck, all those wrong turns and mistakes, also connects the moments you've been happiest, when you've laughed, when you've been applauded, when you've felt proud of yourself, when you've woken from the best sleep of your life, when the sun has shined, when you've felt loved, when you've stood and stared in awe at the stars. Everything in your life – good, bad and everywhere in between, has a single connecting fibre running through it all. And what is even more amazing is that you can wield total control over this common denominator, if only you would choose to do so.

The thing that has brought you to this moment, right now, with everything the way it is, can either be allowed to carry on as it has done for your entire life so far, keeping you stuck in your rut, unhappy, unmotivated, uninspired, delivering results that are much less than satisfactory. Or it can be used to do things differently, to bring new results, results that are better than anything you've experienced before. But the only way to do that is to recognise what that simple thing is, and then to take charge of it. And by taking charge of this one thing that has lead you to where you are today, you will be able to steer yourself to a much better place tomorrow.

This common thread that exists at the middle of this pile of circumstances both fortunate or otherwise, that links all the events and situations in your life, is you.

You are the reason your life sucks. You are the reason things don't go your way. And you are the reason you can't 'deal with it'. You are the reason for all the failures, all the embarrassing moments, all the guilt, all the regret, for your weight issues, for your remorse issues, for not earning what you want, for not being funny, or clever, or popular, or successful.

You are the thing that's been holding you back. You are

the thing that stopped you getting those good grades, that promotion, from meeting the partner of your dreams, from having the nice car, the big house, the big muscles, the shelf full of sporting trophies. You are the thing that has got you here, to where you are right now. And it's up to you whether you stay here, or whether you move forward.

This isn't some sort of shame game or tough love. These things, all the things that make you feel resentful, depressed and anxious about yourself, they're not the only thing you're responsible for. You're also responsible for everything that's gone right in your life. The good exam results, the times you made someone laugh, the times you've really earned that paycheque, the joy you've brought to others and to yourself, the proud moments, the happy moments, the sunny moments. You are the thing that connects all your successes, the times you've felt good about yourself, the times you made someone else feel good about themselves, your good deeds, your accomplishments, the good things in your life.

It's not because of your circumstance, where you were born, the colour of your skin, your height, dietary habits, that thing that happened years ago. It's because of you. The only thing you have any control over is you, and believe it or not, you can have a massive impact on your situation. And your situation can either be perfect, or there could be room for improvement. And, judging by the fact you're reading this, there is probably a lot of room for improvement.

Of course, there are some things that are completely

outside your control. You can't control if it's going to rain tomorrow, but you can certainly decide if you're going to get wet. You can't control if you're going to get hit by a bus tomorrow, but you can look both ways when you cross the street. You can't control the circumstances you were born into, but you can decide if you're going to stay there or if you're going to work to change your situation. You can't control if you're going to get hit by lightning but… ok maybe you really can't control that, but you can influence 90 percent of what happens in your life. But because it feels like everything is stacked against you – and possibly always has been – right now you are probably having a hard time believing it.

But when you realise that you are in charge of you, that the direction you can turn at any given moment is entirely up to you, then you can begin to see that you are in the perfect position to change everything. And I mean everything. You can turn it all around. You can live a happier life, you can achieve goals and dreams, you can earn more money, you can be fitter, slimmer. You can even be blonder – although being taller might be tricky unless you wear platform soles – you can do and be anything you want. But again, the key to this is that it's down to you. No-one else is going to do this for you. Only you can make this happen. As the Buddhist saying goes "I can show you the door, but you must walk through it".

When you start to realise just how much power you hold, you will also begin to see that you've had this power all along. All this time you've been learning and developing and gaining the experiences, skills and understanding that make you not only one of a kind, but give you the unique ability to shape your reality the way you want it, to become a master of the graceful art of living, and to revel in the joy to be found in the life that 'just is'. You will learn how to 'deal with it', to own it, and go far beyond and become extraordinary.

By starting this book you've already taken the first step along the road of transformation. You can live a better life, and be a better version of yourself, with more of the things you want, and less of the stresses you don't. It will happen through four transformations, and you will need to work at all of them. It will be hard, but not as hard as you think. It will take a long time, but not as long as you think. And if you focus on the process and let go of the outcomes, then the outcomes will look after themselves and you will get immense satisfaction from the mastery of the mundane.

The four transformations are:

1. Transformation of perspective
2. Transformation of thought
3. Transformation of emotional reaction
4. Transformation of action

These four transformations don't stand alone from each other, but overlap and merge at their boundaries. Perspective and thought are intertwined and co-related. Thought and emotional reaction hold hands and influence each other. And by the time we get to the fourth transformation, the transformation of action, you'll find that you've already been taking action towards a better life and a better you. Because these transformations are so interwoven, to enjoy the maximum benefits of one transformation it's important to go through them all. And when you do, you will experience a final transformation:

5. Transformation of results

It won't happen overnight, although you will begin to see the benefits pretty quickly. And at its heart lies a practice that you must commit to for the rest of your life if you wish to enjoy the gains to be had. Over time you will adapt and adjust this practice to suit your own personal way of living, you'll create new practices, dispense with old ones that no longer serve you, but all will embrace the idea of taking small positive steps, done consistently over a period of time to create big, noticeable results. And the longer you commit to this practice, the more it will evolve to suit your needs, the more you will incorporate it into yourself and your daily routine, the more powerful it will become and, in turn, the more powerful you will become.

You will begin to see results very early on, but that won't mean your work is done. Indeed, the work is, in itself, a new way of living, a new way of thinking, and a new way of existing. It doesn't end, and it mustn't end. It is the process, and the process is the point.

CHAPTER 2: ONE DROP AT A TIME

"The good life is a process, not a state of being. It is a direction, not a destination." – Carl Rogers

I was a van driver. On the early shift, I would get up at 3am. On the late shift, I would get home at one or two o'clock in the morning. At the beginning of each shift I would arrive at the depot, get in my van and hit the road, transporting groceries to customers who chose to order their weekly shop online and have it delivered to their home.

I was travelling all over the south of England. Seven hours and more than a hundred miles of driving each day. Sometimes I would deliver to a top floor flat in the middle of the city, sometimes I'd be driving my van down narrow lanes to farms in the middle of the countryside. On an easy day, I'd have sixteen deliveries – or drops – to make before I could head back to the depot. On hard days, I could do up to thirty drops, one house after another, one tower block after another, one farm, one cottage, one mansion, relentless, no time to stop and think, no time to wonder how I got here. I never thought for a minute that this was where I'd end up.

I needed the money. I needed to pay the rent. I needed a job. And this was the only job I could get.

I made the decision early on not to hate the job. It is

what it is, I thought, and the moment I started to hate it I knew it would become torture. But some days it really felt like torture. Customers could be rude, parking could be impossible, and trying to reverse a van down a narrow country lane without putting dent in it – a van that was ten feet tall, eight feet wide and twenty-five feet long, weighing nearly four tonnes – took time. And this job was all about time.

Customers were promised their delivery within a one-hour slot. I could be expected to do five or six drops within a single slot, and my sat nav displayed the expected time of arrival, and the number of minutes it would take to get there. I prayed that the customer would be home when I got to their address, that their house was easy to find, that I could park the van without wasting time, that there were no problems with their order, no spillages or leakages, nothing that would cost me a minute or two. Nothing that would make you late for the next drop, and the one after that.

Constantly seeing the minutes tick past, eager to get to the next drop before the numbers on the clock changed, I was watching my life ticking away. One minute at a time.

Each shift generally lasted the same amount of time. If I had thirty drops they would be close together. If I had 16 drops there were greater distances to travel between them. Either way, the temptation was to count them off, one at a time. One drop done, 29 to go. Two drops done, 28 to go. Three drops done… drop, drop, drop, drop.

Like the drops of water that, one by one, over millions of years, wore a groove in the earth that eventually became the Grand Canyon, aiming for that final result, focusing on returning to the depot with an empty van and the eventual journey home made the shift never-ending. Intolerable. Like the drop, drop, drop of water torture, wearing me down in the same way that water wore the Grand Canyon into the earth.

Too often we focus on the ending, on the goal, and every day that we don't get there the frustration builds. We feel ourselves enduring each day, tired and miserable, we count the minutes impatiently, hoping that around the corner we will find the things that we're wishing into our lives, when all we're really doing is wishing our lives away. And the clock ticks and the minutes pass, excruciatingly.

But in the van I learned a secret – if you want to call it that – to reach my goal almost effortlessly. Like magic I could sail through thirty deliveries, and come out the other side with a smile on my face, rather than feeling tired, and worn out and beaten. I learned a technique that helped me to not endure, but to breeze through as many deliveries as the job would throw at me. I could climb staircase after staircase, navigate difficult country lane or congested motorway as if it was a walk in the park. I would carry nearly a tonne of shopping to door after door each day and come away feeling more enlightened after each customer I met.

Rather than wearing me down, each day made me stronger.

This secret I learned – the technique – isn't anything new. It's been around for thousands of years, and is at the very heart of many spiritual philosophies, like Buddhism and Stoicism. It is the same principle behind the successful achievement of anything worthwhile or great. It is the same approach that can turn a coach potato into a marathon runner, a first-grade student into a college graduate, a pauper into a millionaire, or a pile of bricks into a new house. Anything that seems insurmountable can be conquered in the same way that I managed to breeze through those tough shifts, and still reach my goal of getting home at the end of my day without feeling beaten.

The secret, the technique, the way that I got through thirty drops is that I forgot about the thirtieth drop, and focused on the first. I gave it my full attention. In the minute or two I spent with my first customer I attempted to brighten their day, maybe learn something, make my delivery and get back in the van.

Then I focused on my second drop. I gave it my full attention. I greeted my second customer as if they were my first, attempted to brighten their day, made my delivery and then I got back in the van.

Then I focused on my third drop. Then my fourth. Then my fifth. With each drop I lived in the moment, the present, and I focused on the process. I didn't count down the drops. I didn't focus on the end goal. But in doing so the end goal came sooner than I thought, and I went home after a hard day's work, without being beaten by the job. Without hating it, but having mastered it instead.

I simply focused on the process. On the road in front of me. On the drop I was doing at that moment.

Be here now.

This isn't a clumsy metaphor. This is an illustration of how to reach your goal. It's not about waiting, it's about being patient, being calm and focusing on the present. Create your goal, decide your route, and concentrate on the journey. It applies to any objective in life as much as it applies to breezing through a shift of thirty drops on your own in the middle of the countryside before the sun has come up. The journey is as important as the destination – often more so. The process is as important as the goal and, eventually, the process becomes the goal.

If you focus on running a marathon the very first time you put on a pair of running shoes, it will seem impossible. Just focus on leaving the house and taking those first steps, on the process of running. Don't focus on the finished house when you're faced with a pile of bricks, just lay the first brick and learn to love the process of laying each one to the best of your ability. Don't focus on becoming a scientist when you haven't yet learned to read, just focus on A is for Apple and try to absorb as much knowledge as you can.

And it's the same when you learn how to 'deal with it'. When you struggle to lift the duvet in the morning and feel buried under a pile of failure, disappointment, and anxiety, and life seems like something that just happens to you, stop and set yourself the goal of owning your existence and your future. And then focus on the process. Focus on taking the first step, and then taking the second step. As you focus on the process of laying each individual brick as well as you possibly can, before long you will have built your house, and you won't even notice the many thousands of bricks that you've laid perfectly behind you. If you focus on learning to run and the joy of being a runner, you will run marathon after marathon.

This book and the power of living gracefully are exactly the same. A series of steps that will start you off on the road of not just learning to 'deal with it', but to taking ownership of your life. It starts here, but it doesn't end on the last page. This is just the first drop, and as you focus on this and the many more to follow, before long you'll have reached your goal, and you'll be on your way to the next. You will have carved out your own Grand Canyon with a power that comes from within. It's already there, just waiting for you to discover it. It's already within you, and it has been all along. And by engaging with the process of living gracefully you will find it, hold on to it, and nurture it until you feel it running through every strand of your life.

Just remember to focus on the right now, to be present in this moment, and to give it your full attention and best effort. Know your goal and have faith that by getting stuck in to the process you will reach it. The rest will look after itself.

So, let's start at the beginning. The first thing you need to do on this journey of transformation is change your perspective.

CHAPTER RECAP

While it's vital that you have a goal, the process of reaching it as just as important – if not more so. If you focus too much on the result, it can seem ever distant, and impossible to reach. It's better, then, to let go of the goal and instead focus on and fall in love with the process. And the goal will look after itself.

Be here now – and you will be there in the future.

CHAPTER 3: WHOSE GLASSES ARE YOU WEARING?

"If you want to view paradise, simply go ahead and view it."
– Willy Wonka

Every step you take in life, everything you do, every interaction you have with others, with the world around you, and even with the thoughts in your own mind, influences how you perceive the world. We've already discussed how life 'just is', but if your experience has been one of cruelty or missed opportunities you may perceive life to be unfair or harsh. You may see the world as an unkind place, full of cruelty and unpleasant experiences. If, however, you have had a blessed upbringing and good fortune at every turn, you may see the world as full of happiness, success and warmth.

A policeman may see a world full of crime, because that's their experience of it. A nurse may see a world full of illness and disease, because that's their experience of it. A fisherman may see a world of water, while someone living in the desert may see a world of sand.

Your experience of life fundamentally affects your perspective of the world – your world – and whether you realise it or not, you have been programmed to experience the world this way. If you've had a life of constant reassurance, support and affirmation then your programming is likely to be largely positive. If you've had a life of criticism, hardship and cruelty, your programming is likely to be largely negative. If you were to believe everything you read in the newspaper you'd think murderers were waiting on every street corner, but if you watched only the Disney channel, you'd think the world was full of unicorns and fairy tales.

If you're not where you want to be in life, the likelihood is you have negative programming, based on negative experiences, which have led to less than desirable results. Your programming influences the way you interpret the external and internal stimuli that you're constantly receiving, and this interpretation influences your perspective. Your perspective is unique to you, and can be influenced by your upbringing, your ethics and morals, the music you listen to, the people you hang out with, the way you talk to yourself, the newspapers you read – in fact your perspective is constantly growing, evolving and changing and feeds off every experience you ever have, both internal and external. It is a huge presence in your life – but the funny thing is, just like the air which you need to breathe, and just like light which you need to see, it's invisible until you train yourself to recognise it.

But it's there, and it plays a massive role in the way you experience the world, and the way you live life. Believe it or not, the difference between you and the person down the road who's appears to be doing much better in life could simply be a matter of perspective.

You need to reprogram your outlook with some positive biases, and undo years and years of negative programming. You can't venture down any road when all you see are dead ends. So, get yourself out of this cul-de-sac and try to change how you see the world.

We'll start with a handy metaphor:

Picture the humble bumble bee. That happy little black and yellow chap, buzzing a busy little tune as he floats from colourful flower to colourful flower on a beautiful summer day, before heading back to the hive full of other happy bees, where he'll make lots of sweet, golden, delicious honey for you to spread on your toast for breakfast.

You couldn't have a more positive, happy scene if you tried, right? In fact, the image of that bee happily going about its work even conjures up the warmth of a summer day. You can almost taste that amber nectar, it's such a vivid, happy image.

But what if you were allergic to bee stings? What if, as a child, you'd been stung by a bee and gone into anaphylactic shock, been rushed to hospital in the back of an ambulance with your terrified parents right next to you, to receive an emergency injection of epinephrine by the doctors, bringing you back from the very brink of death? How would you see the bee then?

Chances are that same bee wouldn't appear as such a happy little chap, buzzing his upbeat tune as he went from flower to flower collecting pollen to give us delicious honey. Instead you'd view that bee as nothing short of a flying death machine on a mission to kill! You'd probably start to panic, flapping your arms around to get him away from you, and you'd run a mile before anyone would have known what was going on. And in all that flapping around the startled bee may well have stung you anyway.

But the thing is, it's exactly the same bee in both scenarios. Nothing's changed other than your perspective, which is based on an earlier experience. The bee 'just is'.

Life 'just is'. And you can either enjoy the honey, or be stung to death.

My sister owned a little black cat. She loved this cat, and it loved her. She'd adopted it from a rescue centre, and lavished it with a loving home, plenty of food and attention and it returned the affection with lots of purring and plenty of cat love! But this cat was terrified of men, and in particular, men's feet. If you were a man there was no chance the cat would let you stroke it, and it would rarely even come in the same room as you. It would simply cower in the corner until you left.

You don't need to be an animal psychologist to understand the kind of life this cat must have had before my sister adopted it. Imagine what kind of abuse you would have to go through to have such a terrible fear of men's feet imprinted permanently on your mind like that. You don't need to have it spelled out to get a good understanding of the kind of treatment the poor animal experienced at the hands (or feet) of its previous owner.

But we're exactly like that cat. When we find ourselves in a position where we're unhappy, full of self-loathing, broke, a failure, it's because we've allowed the repeated kicking that we've taken throughout our lives to imprint upon us. When we fail time and time again, what outcomes are we going to expect? When someone tells us we're no good day in and day out, we start to believe it.

To make matters worse, this programming affects the way we behave, the way we interact with the world. When we think of ourselves as failures, we don't even try to succeed. And when we don't try something we have already immediately failed, as ice hockey player Wayne Gretzky famously observed when he said, "you miss 100 per cent of the shots you don't take."

When we think we're not good enough, we act without confidence, and the results we experience reflect this. When we fly into a panic at the sight of that bee and start waving our arms around in terror, we increase our chances of being stung. When we feel like our endeavours are going to come to nothing, we stop trying. When we have our ability to make decisions taken away from us, we stop making them. We become disempowered. Our potential goes unrealised.

Our experience affects how we see the world, which affects how we interact with the world, which in turn affects our outcomes. This then reinforces our programming and the cycle starts again, creating an ever-decreasing negative feedback loop. Before long life starts to become something that simply happens to us. We feel like we have no control, no matter how hard we try, even though the entire reason things have ended up like this is because we've allowed it to happen.

Don't get me wrong – when you are repeatedly told you're worthless, or undermined, or blocked from making decisions or even just 'doing' or 'being', it wears you down and your perspective of the world and of yourself changes. Yes, you allowed it to happen. But yes, you may have been too young to know otherwise, or too disempowered to stand up for yourself, or the negative input might have been so imperceptibly small, or the negative comment so throw-away and without malice or intent, that you may not even have noticed it at the time.

The transformation that you're now undertaking isn't about blaming yourself or anyone else for why you got here. Fixating on the past serves no purpose other than to fuel more paralysing negativity, more guilt, more bitterness and anxiety. The transformation is about recognising that the future can be better – that you can be better – and you have the power to make it that way. While your actions (or lack thereof) in the past have brought you to this point, by engaging in small, almost effortless positive actions, you can take back control of your life.

And when you start to take back control, it doesn't take long before you notice small changes for the better, and then something profound begins to happen. At first, you simply aim to make small changes by taking small actions. The magic of taking these small actions is that it doesn't take long for them to compound and turn into something much bigger. And when you see these changes, when you first notice them happening, you will finally begin to recognise the power that you actually have over your own life. Rather than being a victim of a life that merely happens to you, you start to realise that you can be an active participant in it. When you see how you can change your perspective, and how big a deal that is, you will begin to appreciate your ability to create change and achieve things that you had previously thought impossible.

Yet all you are doing is taking small positive steps. So small that they take very little effort, but begin to undo the equally small negative steps that got you into this situation – this state – in the first place. It takes no effort to eat a greasy beef burger. But if you eat one for every meal, every day, before long you'll notice the impact on your wellbeing. Similarly, it takes no effort not to eat a greasy beef burger, and the reverse becomes true.

It works the same way when it comes to undoing the negative biases that have built-up, layer upon layer over your lifetime to have such a huge impact on your perspective. Like sediment they've settled down until they've created the person you are now. But layer by layer, they can also be undone and replaced with something much better, much more effective. It's still you, but it's a better version of you.

Another metaphor coming up: Imagine wearing a pair of sunglasses. We've all done this on a sunny day, and at first it makes everything darker, but before long your eyes become accustomed to this new filter and you see the world as it is. At least you think you do.

Imagine, though, that it's a particularly bright day, and you put on your sunglasses. After a little while your eyes become accustomed to the dark filter of the lenses and you forget you're wearing them at all. But on this day the sunlight is really bright, so you reach for another pair of sunglasses and you put them on over the top of the last pair. Eventually your eyes adjust to this second filter, and again you forget you're even wearing sunglasses.

But still the sun is incredibly bright, so you reach for yet another pair of sunglasses and you slip them on. Only, this time, the glasses are designed for someone with bad eyesight, and not only do they make your view of the world darker but they distort it as well. Your brain and your eyes are miracles of evolution, so they soon learn to cope with these new lenses, and again you forget you're wearing them. Time after time you put on more and more sunglasses. You don't realise it but your view of the world is so distorted that what you're seeing is nothing like reality, yet you have become so accustomed to these filters that you're none the wiser. You just think that's what the world looks like.

Wearing all these lenses, you think you're doing ok, but the reality is that your worldview is so distorted that in truth you're stumbling along, tripping over things, avoiding obstacles that aren't there, bumping into obstacles that you can't see, and generally wobbling along out of control.

Every experience you have is like putting on another pair of sunglasses, another pair of lenses. Sometimes they help you see more clearly, sometimes they distort your perspective so you only see the bad things, and miss the good stuff altogether.

When things don't go your way, it becomes easy to focus on the negative because, well, that's all you can see through your many lenses and filters. You have developed a bias, and this has informed your behaviour, your results and even your personality. But you can use the idea of bias to your advantage, to change your perspective. You can literally make the decision to take off all these sunglasses and filters, and see the world differently. And if you can see the world differently, you can interact with it differently. While the world won't have changed one little bit, you can influence the results you experience, you can change yourself and your life, simply by changing your biases and your perspective. You can take off the sunglasses that don't serve you, and replace them with lenses that do.

Try this exercise: Think of a yellow car. It doesn't need to be any more specific than that. Simply get the idea of a yellow car into your head. Now, over the next few days keep a mental tally of how many times you see a yellow car as you go about your business. Chances are you'll start seeing a lot more of them than you did before, and you'll see them in the most unexpected places. It's almost as if suddenly you're attracting yellow cars into your life.

This is a type of attention bias, and you've spent your life biased towards negativity, towards failure, towards the things that prove you're not good enough, and if you keep seeing the world in this way you are destined for a life of unhappiness, failure and mediocrity. Your sunglasses allow you to see only the things that don't work out for you – you are literally tuned in to negativity. And the more you focus on that, the more it seems to be attracted to you. Just like the yellow cars.

But what if you could instead focus on opportunities, or the things that make life wonderful, or all the things that go right, or that make you feel good about yourself? What if you could attract good things into your life?

Well, you can, and you can start doing it right now. Next time you're at the shops, get yourself a notebook and a pen. It doesn't have to be a fancy notebook, but it helps if it's a nice one, as this notebook is going to become a major tool for changing your perspective from a negative one to a positive one. And as a result, it's going to change the way you interact with the world, and therefore the results you see in your life.

Once a day, you're going to put aside some time to write in this notebook all the positive things that happened to you that day. If the only time you can spare is in the morning before breakfast, then it will be all the positive things that happened to you the previous day. But the thing is, this is an exercise that you must commit to doing every day, and you must make that commitment right now. This exercise will become part of your routine, and it will become the foundation for turning your life around.

The small, almost infinitesimal amount of effort required to write in this notebook is the thing that will get the ball rolling, and start to turn your negative life into a positive one. Even the busiest people can spare the few minutes it takes to do this exercise every day. You can do it before you turn off the light at bedtime.

You can do it on the bus on the way to work. You can even do it while you're waiting for the kettle to boil. A few minutes to write down ten positive things from your day. That's all it takes, and there are no excuses. As Shia LaBoeuf says: "DO IT".

So, get your notebook, and start writing, but you mustn't forget the rules.

"Rules?" I hear you exclaim. "You never mentioned rules."

Of course there are rules. There are always rules. But these simple rules will make this exercise even more effective and powerful than you ever thought possible.

1. Each day you must write down ten positive experiences from the day before. They could be something small like the smell of your first cup of coffee in the morning, the feeling of your favourite sweater, or even the theme tune to your favourite television show. Alternatively, it could be something as complicated or as epic as completing a business deal, finishing a chapter in a book, learning a new word in a foreign language, getting a promotion at work. Anything that gives you a sense of satisfaction, makes you feel good, or in some way, big or small, adds a bit of a smile to your day.

2. Keep it positive. You're not allowed to write things in your journal like "I was really pleased I got the last seat on the bus and made that rude man stand" or "I felt satisfied that I got a better

score in the exam than Steve, because he's an idiot." Keep it wholesome, positive and good natured. Similarly, avoid negative words and phrases like: didn't, can't, won't, shouldn't, not, isn't, wouldn't etc. Phrase things so that you're using the most positive words and phrases possible. Instead of writing "I'm glad I didn't fall over", rephrase it as "I'm happy I stayed standing." Put as much energy into making not only the things you're writing, but also the way you're writing them, as positive and as wholesome as possible.

3. You should write ten new things every day. You can't write about that first cup of coffee every day because the exercise will lose its power. You need to force yourself to really think about ten different things, no matter how big or small, so that your brain starts to develop that positive attention bias. Even if it's something as mundane as the lovely feeling of putting on a new pair of socks in the morning, get it down on paper. Nothing is too small for the positivity notebook.

4. Don't tell anyone else you're doing this – at least not at first. This is your exercise, and yours alone. It's very easy for other people to cast judgement on what you're doing, to roll their eyes and undo the hard work before it's even begun. Keep it to yourself for now.

5. Do it every day. No excuses.

The thing about keeping a positivity journal like this on a daily basis, is that it forces you to focus on the good stuff. Even if you've had a crappy day, by doing this journal and really focusing on the things that went right, or that made you feel good, or that brought you even the slightest bit of pleasure, you are starting to reprogram your mind to see positivity everywhere. You'll start to hunt for things that make you feel good so you can write them in your book, and you'll tune in to the good things, putting less emphasis on the bad. After a while, everywhere you go you'll be looking for stuff you enjoy, sights, sounds, smells, interactions, conversations, feelings, experiences. You might enjoy a good meal, feel the warmth of the sun on your face, hear the birds singing, catch up with an old friend, get a seat on the bus, receive some good feedback on a piece of work. You'll start looking for it everywhere, and you'll start to find it everywhere.

I like to write my positivity journal at the end of the day before I go to bed. I keep my notebook on the bedside table, and before I go to sleep I spend five minutes quickly listing things that have brought a bit of sunshine to my day. Even if I had a dressing down from my boss, there's always that tasty dinner I had, or that conversation with a friend, or that beautiful sunset on my drive home, or the sound of birds singing outside my window. Even if I drove my car into a ditch, there was the smile on the recovery vehicle driver's face, the sounds of the countryside around me, or learning that the car wasn't as badly damaged as I feared. Every day you must look for positive things to write in your book.

The very act of writing these things in the notebook, and phrasing them in the most positive way possible becomes a positive experience. And what's more, the little notebook becomes a symbol of positivity in itself. Just having it there, overflowing with days, weeks and months of positive experiences gives it a positive vibe all its own. It becomes like a comfort blanket. Something that radiates positivity and helps you focus on the good stuff, even when you think there isn't any.

These positive things, no matter how small, are the things you need to be thankful for, grateful for, and a practice of gratitude can underpin a change in your perspective for the better. And that is the first step to a better life.

If you're struggling to find positive things in your life, things to be grateful for, then I would like to offer this story, from the life of actor Stephen Tobolowsky, a fine American actor who you will recognise as the man who played Ned Ryerson in the film Groundhog Day. Tobolowsky recounted his story of the 'Shamah' during an interview with James Altucher, and you don't need to be religious to appreciate it.

Tobolowsky was about to travel to Canada to make a movie, and he went to visit his Rabbi at the synagogue to ask how he could take his Judaism with him when he travelled. His Rabbi told him to say the Shamah twice a day. The Jehovah Shamah is a prayer in Judaism that roughly translates as "God is there". After saying it twice day for a week, his Rabbi instructed him to start saying the Shamah every time he received an unexpected blessing. But Tobolowsky didn't make it to the end of the first day before he found himself saying it all the time, as he explained during the interview:

"When the plane didn't crash in Canada, I said the Shamah. When I got through the immigration line quickly, I said the Shamah. I got to the hotel room and I had a TV with a working remote – SHAMAH! But the curling championships were on the television, so no Shamah there! I went to eat dinner in an Italian restaurant and the owner recognised me from a movie I'd been in and gave me a free bottle of wine – SHAMAH! I had a snowflake in my cup of coffee in the morning. Shamah. Morning to night I realised I was the most blessed person on earth."

I'm not saying you have to be thankful for everything, but it's a good example of how, even on the darkest of days, there are things to be positive about. Look hard enough and you'll find something to put in your notebook. Do it daily, and you'll find you don't need to look that hard at all. And after a while you'll become tuned in to the positive things around you. You'll start behaving in a much more upbeat manner and rather than flailing your arms about in fear of getting stung, you'll be open to the idea that maybe, just maybe, the bumble bee is a happy little chap after all.

Positivity is like a muscle, and the more you use it the stronger it becomes. But this positivity practice has two big flaws that you need to be aware of from the start, otherwise it's likely you'll get off to a good start only to find yourself back where you started later.

The first flaw is that this exercise is really easy to do,

just like not eating a greasy burger. It requires very little effort on your part to write down ten things that make you feel good every day, especially when the positivity muscle starts getting stronger and you become more tuned in to the positive aspects of the world around you. And because it takes very little effort, it's also very easy to abandon the practice. It's such a small thing to do each day, that it becomes easy to skip a day, and then eventually to stop doing it altogether. It's important that you dedicate yourself to the practice of writing your list every day, and doing so in the most positive language possible because the moment you stop, just like a muscle, all that good work will start to atrophy come undone. That small positive input will very easily be replaced by small negative inputs, and before long, layer by layer, you'll be back to where you were before.

The second thing to understand about this positivity practice is that you build up a tolerance to it. This is why it's important to write down different things every day, so that you keep it engaging and enjoyable. The more you do it, the more of a hunger you'll feel for the buzz it gives you, and the harder it will be to maintain that same blissed-out feeling that you get when you started.

But this is just the start. As we progress through the rest of the book the daily practice will grow and change as we build upon this foundation and eventually you'll learn techniques to keep it fresh, try new things, and let it adapt and evolve to suit you personally. Get stuck in, commit now to giving it all your effort, and stay the course.

By focusing on the positive you start to see how much your perspective can affect the world around you. In reality the world is just as it was before, you're just seeing it in a better light, with a better pair of sunglasses. With just a tiny bit of effort, repeated consistently, you will become aware of how your internal state affects your experience of the world, and you will develop the ability to change yourself, to improve yourself, and take control of your inner dialogue.

Of course, there will still be things that don't go in your favour, things that don't work out right. You'll get stuck in traffic, get a dressing down from your boss, stub your toe, knock things over, or worse. But by doing this exercise, and in particular by learning how to rephrase what you write in the most positive way possible, you are beginning to develop a skill that will enable you to reframe things that might appear to be negative in a more positive way.

For example, when a piece of work gets rejected, you can see it as an opportunity to see where you went wrong and where you can improve. When you miss your train – yet again – it's an opportunity to see where in your routine you could change something to make sure you always get to the station on time. When you get stuck in traffic you could use it as an opportunity to listen to an audiobook and learn something new. When things don't go your way, it gives you a chance to make small, almost unnoticeable improvements to your life so that you can get it right next time.

Even when things that are beyond your control don't

go in your favour, it's a chance for you to reassess your situation, your practices and behaviours to see how you could be better prepared should the same thing happen again. Suddenly, you're not simply tuned in to the good stuff that's going on around you, but you're also able to see the bad things in a more positive light. And by practicing this daily, and keeping in mind how you would normally have reacted to a situation but how you're now taking control of it, you're developing the ability to interrupt your previous programming. You are taking control, and later in the book we'll talk more about interrupting our programming to take ownership of our selves and our lives.

This is just the beginning. Keep up the practice and you'll find joy in a blue sky, in traffic, in sights, sounds and smells. Even a rainy walk to the shops can become a pleasurable experience as you look out for things that bring you happiness and you recognise what even the smallest amount of pleasure feels like. You'll start to feel empowered as you begin to realise that you have control over how you respond to even the worst things that happen. This feeling becomes amplified, you become blissed out, tuned in to everything that glitters around you.

When you begin to see the benefit in every outcome no matter how good or bad it may previously have seemed, it will appear that everything is starting to go your way. But your perspective isn't just about looking at the outside world, it's also about the way you look at yourself and the way you talk internally. After all, you are at the centre of your Universe, and for too long you've been driving on autopilot, bumping from one negative experience to another, so it's time to write your story and decide your outcome.

Can you change your self-view? Is it possible to see yourself in a much more positive light just as you can tune in to the positivity around you? Can you go from feeling like a loser with nothing to offer, from someone bent double from carrying a lifetime of baggage, to someone filled with positive energy, who feels good about themselves, what they're capable of and what they can bring to the world? And can you turn that energy into action that can improve your life and yourself immeasurably?

Of course you can, but it takes work, and time, and a commitment to keep going. You need to become self-aware, and you need to take charge of your control centre. But most importantly you need to take charge of how you think and how you feel. And just as you changed your perspective of the world around you, you can use the power you gain from taking small positive steps to take ownership of yourself, your mental processes and your self-talk.

CHAPTER RECAP

Your perspective is influenced by every experience you've ever had. If you have a negative perspective you will see the world differently than if you have a positive perspective. But you can reprogram yourself to see things more positively by actively seeking out and focusing on the positive things in your life – and yourself – and by giving them more attention and energy than the negative things.

CHAPTER 4: THOUGHTS AREN'T FACTS

"Be a force of love as often as you can and turn away negative thoughts whenever you feel them surface." – Dr. Wayne Dyer

I was an editor in New York, producing a glossy magazine about design. My first book had just been published, and I was living the dream. But the problem with living the dream is that when you're living it, it doesn't feel like a dream. It feels very much like normal life. Of course, there were times when I felt special. Being an Englishman in New York got me a lot of attention and made me some wonderful friends. But I still had to get up and walk to work every day. I still had to make ends meet on a meagre journalist's salary. I still had to feed myself. Wash my clothes. Go to the bathroom. No one ever goes to the toilet in movies.

For most of my day I was sat in front of a computer, writing features, editing features, commissioning features, commissioning photographers, commissioning illustrators, sending emails, and working on my second book.

One of the key skills you need when you're working with words on a computer is the ability to type. I learned to type at a young age, as I'd been an early adopter of the personal home computer, and I'm rather proud of my typing speed. I could interview somebody on the telephone and type out the transcript in real time, as the conversation was taking place. People always seem impressed with the size of my wpm!

It's all down to practice, and I've had lots of practice navigating a keyboard. Just like a pianist knows where his fingers are meant to be to create a particular sound on the piano, I know, from years and years of training, the movements my hands need to make to take the words in my head and make them appear on the screen. Anyone who is good at typing will know exactly what I mean, as will anyone who has spent years playing a musical instrument. With practice we can teach our hands to do pretty much anything.

Look at your hands. Do it right now. Wonderfully versatile appendages, they have evolved over millions of years to give us the dexterity to do an infinite number of complex things. With our hands we can lay bricks and build a house. We can shake the hand of another person as a greeting. We can clap and applaud a virtuoso performance (also played using hands). We can write a letter to a loved one. We can carry out science experiments. We can draw schematics for space rockets that will take mankind to the moon, and then we can use our hands to build them and fly them. We can feel how hot things are, what a texture is like, we can grasp things, throw things, type things and sew things.

Our hands and our ability to manipulate the world around us separates us from our closest relatives, the apes. Our hands have put mankind on top of the tallest mountain, at the bottom of the deepest ocean, they've built machines which have now left our solar system, and placed flowers into the barrels of guns.

There's seemingly nothing our hands can't do. But imagine if you sat down at your desk, a clean sheet of paper in front of you with the intention of writing that letter to a loved one. As you reach for the pen, instead of picking it up, your hand slaps you around the face instead. Again you reach for the pen, and again you get a slap around the face. Each time you try to write that letter your own hand slaps you around the face. It's a ridiculous notion, but picture it for a moment. Each time you reach for that pen, your own hand prevents you from doing what you want to do, and instead it rears up and gives you a hard slap across the cheek.

Our hands are a part of us, they belong to us, and we expect to be in full control of them. They are infinitely versatile and we can achieve so much with them, but what if they didn't do exactly as we wished, and instead sabotaged us every time we tried to use them, and even when weren't using them would fly up and slap us around the face without any warning? We wouldn't expect it, and we wouldn't allow it. These are our hands and we expect them to do as we command.

It seems daft, the idea of our own hands sabotaging our efforts to do things. Yet, we allow your minds to do this to us all the time. They stop us from trying new things by filling us with fear, by interfering with our personality and by making us feel insecure, anxious and nervous. Our minds tell us that we're not good enough, that people will laugh at us, that we'll only fail. Even when we're in the shower, our minds remind us of that thing we said to that complete stranger at a party five years ago that we really wish we hadn't, or that thing that haunts us from our childhood. Just like the hand slapping us across the face, our minds are sabotaging us, when instead we could be using them as tools to achieve so much more if only they weren't busy making us feel miserable.

The human mind is a miraculous, complex thing. Einstein used his to develop the theory of relativity. Pythagoras used his to unlock the secrets of the triangle. Arthur C. Clarke used his to write stories that take us far into the future. Do we really want ours to be used worrying about what people will think about our new shoes? So much of our mind's capacity is used up undermining us, telling us not to try, pointing out our weaknesses and where we went wrong, when instead it could be used for so much more. We could achieve so many great things if we could just free up the capacity that we waste sabotaging ourselves and making ourselves feel bad. But instead we carry on allowing our minds to slap us across the face. Constantly. Over and over and over again.

But consider this: while our hands are part of us, they are not us. They are a tool that we can use to do things. We can command our hands to grip the steering wheel and navigate us to amazing places. We can learn sign language to communicate with people who don't have the blessing of hearing. We can use our hands to pick an apple from an apple tree. Our hands are limitless tools designed to do our bidding. But they are not us.

Our minds are the same, they are a part of us, but they are not us, and should be considered powerful tools for our use. But instead they distort our perspective of ourselves and the world around us. They feed us untruths, make us worry what people think, make us waste time reading between the lines of what someone might have been saying when they were actually saying something completely different.

Our minds feed our insecurities, stoke the flames of our anxiety, and paralyse us to the point where some days we can hardly bear to get out of bed. They fill up with roadblocks when their capacity could be used to take us on those journeys to amazing places, where we could change the world.

But what if you could step back from the constant chatter of your mind, and say to yourself "thoughts aren't facts"? What if you could interrupt that inner monologue, and say to your mind "these thoughts don't serve me" and think about something else instead?

You can, and I've just shown you how.

It's all about recognising the tricks your mind is playing on you, and interrupting them. Imagine someone was talking to you, telling you what an awful person you are, how you're such a failure and nobody likes you, and how that thing you said to that stranger at the party five years ago may or may not have been misunderstood as a bit of an insult, and now everyone will forever think you're a bad person, and you don't deserve to succeed because you're weak, and you should be ashamed of yourself for not being a better person, and you shouldn't have taken the last bread roll at dinner, and you suck at life because you've got the wrong attitude, and don't even think of applying for that job or starting that project because you'll only fail, and and and...

"SHUT UP!"

You wouldn't let someone stand there and say all those negative, undermining things to you. Those words serve only to stop you in your tracks, make you feel worthless, guilty, anxious. But every day you allow your mind to make you feel guilty about things long past, you allow it to magnify your insecurities, your fears and weaknesses. You allow your mind to find things to worry about even when you have nothing to worry about. When it really is as simple as saying "STOP! These thoughts don't serve me, so I'm going to think about something else."

With a little practice, you can learn to see when these thoughts are occurring, and as soon as you feel them pop up, you can tell them to stop and turn your attention elsewhere. Of course, it helps if you have something else ready to focus your attention on – a project, or something you're looking forward to, working on or planning. If you don't have a project that you can focus your thoughts on, instead focus your thinking on the ten positive things you're going to write in your notebook this evening. Or what you're going to have for dinner. Or how you can improve your life with one little action today. Or who you can help tomorrow. Or even what you watched on television last night.

With practice, you can interrupt these unnecessary negative thoughts before they turn into unnecessary negative emotions. It takes a little while, but with consistent practice over time you will no longer be at the mercy of your mind, you will have taken back the power to use it for better things.

This isn't anything new – it's basic mindfulness 101. It's about being consciously aware of yourself and the space you're in at this very moment. Aware of what you're doing, how it makes you feel, your breathing, your body, and most importantly aware of the thoughts passing through your head. It's about being able to step outside these things and observe them, almost as if they were very much separate from you – witnessing the thoughts as they happen, rather than being one with the thoughts, and therefore emotionally paired to them.

Meditation practices are useful when practising mindfulness, and we will touch on these later in the book, but it's important to understand that this isn't about subjugating your emotions, or keeping things buried beneath the surface. As soon as you start to bury your feelings, just like a volcano pressure will start to build up and over time you can expect an eruption of everything you've been hiding from yourself.

This exercise is instead about understanding that your thoughts are not facts, and that you are not your thoughts. Negative feelings arise when we allow our minds to feed our insecurities, which in turn disempower us and foster negativity in any or all of it's unfortunate forms. It's about saying that we've punished ourselves enough for that bad thing we did or said five years ago, and our time and energy is now better spent forgiving ourselves and becoming better people tomorrow. Rather than allowing your mind to beat you up day in, day out, it's about telling yourself that you're going to take back that capacity and put it to good use building a better life. It's about saying that you deserve better than this, you are more than this, and there are things that you want to do, that you want to think about, and this constant negative self-talk is getting in the way.

I would find my negative self-talk was at its worst when I was in the shower, or stood in front of the mirror shaving. Moments when I was alone, on autopilot, and my mind was wandering. I would start to feel my anxiety growing as my mind leapt from one bad thought to another. And then one day I borrowed a phrase from personal development guru Bob Proctor, and literally said in my head the words "I only give energy to the thoughts that serve me." And in that instant, I took away the energy from my negative mind and reclaimed it for myself. I was tired of not being the best version of myself, of not having ownership of my thoughts, my actions and my life.

I did this, and do this, every time I feel those negative thoughts arising, and I'm able to stop them triggering the negative emotions that paralyse me. And what's amazing is that this same interruption technique can be used to take the power back not just in your head, but in the real world as well.

So get practicing and put this technique into action, because when you start to appreciate its power, you'll realise there's nothing you can't do.

CHAPTER RECAP

Your mind can be constantly buzzing with negative thoughts, which stop you embarking on new adventures, seeing your true worth, and realising your full potential. But the version of the world presented by your mind is a distortion of reality and your inner voice does not always speak the truth. By remembering that thoughts are not facts, that your inner voice is not you, and that your mind is a tool for you to use rather than something that should control you, you can take away its power and regain its full capacity for achieving the things you want to achieve.

CHAPTER 5: MIND THE GAP

"Once you replace negative thoughts with positive ones, you'll start having positive results." – Willie Nelson

Negative thoughts lead to negative feelings. Input leads to output. And, as we've just learned, if we can identify and interrupt the negative thoughts (the input) which don't serve us, then we can take ownership of our feelings (the output). And we can do the same with our negative reactions to external stimuli and as a result become much happier, with reduced stress, and be much more in control of ourselves and the way we behave. And when we do that we can choose to live gracefully, rather than being a puppet at the mercy of our negative emotions.

Have you ever known someone who was always able to 'push your buttons' and make you angry or frustrated or sad? Well, the truth is that whenever you react that way you're giving them power over you, power to trigger an emotional reaction within you. But how much better would it be if you could take back control of those buttons and choose not to react to those provocations at all?

In the same way that you interrupted your non-beneficial negative thoughts in the last chapter so that they were unable to trigger negative emotions and prevent you from working towards your goals, you can also interrupt your own internal processes so that rather than reacting to a situation, you can choose a measured response instead.

You see, it's not the person pushing your buttons who makes you angry, it's you. The anger is coming from within you – it is a part of you – and you can either choose to let that reaction carry on as usual, or you can interrupt it, and choose a much better response instead.

How cool would it be to totally own your own actions rather than letting them own you? Once you understand that it's not the fault of external influences when your emotional reactions are triggered, but rather the result of your own internal processes, you are able to disarm any person or circumstance from holding any power over you. When you understand that you oversee your internal processes – that you are in charge of them – you can choose whether something makes you happy or sad. You can choose to find joy in a cloudless blue sky, and focus on all those things that bring you ecstasy, and you can choose not to react to those things that bring you stress, anxiety, anger, and worry. They are your buttons. It's entirely up to you if you allow others to press them.

These emotions – in nearly all circumstances – have no benefit other than to cause you harm. When you allow someone to 'push our buttons' you do not benefit from getting angry, from allowing your temper to overflow, or by allowing yourself to get upset or feel intimidated or undermined. Pure negative emotional reactions like that don't serve you, so why not choose a measured response that does?

Just as a toddler throws a tantrum and starts kicking and screaming on the floor when they don't get their way – allowing their emotions to take control and do the driving – so you are exactly the same when you lose control and throw a tantrum when things don't go your way. Perhaps a loved one has done that thing that they know winds you up. Perhaps your football team has lost, again, to that much lesser team and you're miserable for days to come. Perhaps your work colleague makes that irritating noise when he eats and you can feel your fists start to tighten, your teeth clench and your blood boil. Perhaps that person who bullies you refuses to stop no matter how much you beg them.

You allow these things to have control over you, you give away your power to them, but what you don't realise is that the entire time the emotional reaction – the itch-like irritation – has been coming from within. You are the one causing yourself to be wound up, and you are the cause of your misery when your team loses or your workmate makes that slurping sound. You can take back the power in all of these situations by simply letting go. Recognise the stimulus (the input), interrupt the usual process, and in doing so create a gap between the input and the usual output. And then decide how to respond (the new output). Take ownership of your inner processes, instead of giving your power away and allowing them to own you.

During my life as a van driver, I learned a lot from the complexities of traffic. On a regular basis, I would see someone pull out too soon from a side road – perhaps an elderly driver – when it would perhaps have been more sensible to wait for a bigger space in the flow of traffic. It wasn't uncommon for the driver into whose path this car had just pulled to take umbrage, pull up right behind the other hapless driver, and then slam on their brakes, beeping their horn and flashing their lights.

Consider the situation. A driver pulls onto the main road, and another driver reacts aggressively (be honest, we've all done it). The result is that both drivers end up stressed by the experience, but neither are any closer to their destination. All that anger, heated emotion, and stress has achieved nothing positive, and has in fact been detrimental to all parties. Just like a toddler throwing a tantrum, that angry driver has given his power away by reacting in an undignified, uncontrolled manner, by allowing his emotions to take the wheel. And he has probably nearly caused an accident in the process, and all to simply try to prove a point. The whole sorry scene is not very graceful, and this book is all about the power of graceful living.

But what if, rather than acting aggressively, the driver had simply taken his foot off the accelerator for a moment, allowing the other car space to pull out without causing a scene. Not only is this a more graceful, elegant response to the same situation, but neither driver is stressed out, nobody's emotions are running out of control, and everyone gets home safely without feeling frightened or anxious.

When you refuse to allow your negative emotions to do the driving by taking your foot off the accelerator and choosing to respond instead of reacting, you can introduce the same calm elegance into all decision making. When you allow only positive emotions to overwhelm you – and even then only at times when you allow it to happen – and prevent the chain reaction that gives your power away and reduces you to the same level as an angry toddler having a tantrum, then you not only improve your effectiveness in your actions, but you remain unflappable in the face of those people and situations that would wish to do you harm or cause you stress. And in the process, you earn the respect of others, and gain self-respect in the process.

When a person, situation or thing could potentially push your buttons and cause a negative reaction, how about you choose instead to take ownership of those buttons rather than allowing them to take ownership of you, by choosing a measured response instead? Or in other words, rather than allowing your power to be taken from you by your emotional reaction, why not choose to retain it and opt for a beneficial response that allows it to grow with grace and elegance instead?

I spent time in Indonesia where a very special man named Bowa sat cross-legged in front of me and attempted to teach me to meditate. I won't go into the finer nuances of meditation, but the basic idea is to close your eyes and focus on your breathing and your posture, and not to let thoughts or the things around you distract you from these two simple things. Simply focus on your breathing and your posture. And in the process, reach clarity of mind so that you can see your thoughts as things that are very separate from you.

When you feel yourself being distracted by the world outside you or the thoughts within you, recognise where your attention is going, and return your focus to your breathing and your posture. Whenever a noise catches your attention, or a thought pops into your head, acknowledge it and return to your posture and your breathing. It's not about stopping the thoughts, it's about letting them pass, and returning your focus to those two other things.

Just posture.

And breathing.

Bowa told me that when you're in the middle of a really good meditation session you could be sat in the pouring rain, with ants crawling all over you, but it wouldn't be enough to distract you from your posture, and your breathing. Now, when I find myself in a situation where I would normally respond in a negative way, where I would become stressed out or angry, I imagine it is just like having ants crawling on me. I acknowledge the presence of the irritation, and then I adjust my posture, take a breath, and take my power back. You can be stronger than all the things that 'push your buttons'. You must simply choose to be.

You can choose your response, if a situation even requires one. You can choose a response that is graceful, a response that is you at your very best. You can choose to let the rain pour on you and accept it elegantly and with measure, with calmness and kindness and thoughtfulness. You can let those harmless ants carry on their journey, and as they cause you no harm you, in turn, cause them no harm.

Or you can react. You can choose the poor option,

cause yourself stress and anxiety and worry, and inflict it on others as well. You can curse the rain, and flee to a dry place tripping and falling into a puddle in the process. You can leap to your feet in a frenzy and squash the harmless ants who are really causing no bother at all, and cause them to bite you. You can speed up behind the old man in the car, flashing your lights, beeping your horn and causing stress to both him and yourself, and possibly causing you both to crash. And you can let your colleague with the noisy chewing stop you from effectively getting on with your job.

The choice is yours. But if you strive to be better, more effective, the best version of yourself, you can create a gap between the external input and your external output. You can go to the effort of choosing a response instead of a submitting to a reaction. And the truth is, it's really no effort at all.

By interrupting the input/output process, so that you can control the output, it can empower you to start each new moment afresh, rather than dragging a negative reaction with you throughout the whole day, infecting everything you touch with sour negativity. You can start again, anew, with a refreshed effectiveness and a renewed productivity.

You can press reset.

Imagine President Obama sitting in the war room at the White House. Faced with a grave responsibility of deciding to take military action and order an air strike on a target that will, without doubt, result in the loss of human life. And then moments later he would be required to appear smiling and cheery for a photocall with a group of schoolchildren? All day long he had to move from one situation to another, but whatever the gravity of the last moment, he couldn't let his emotional response spill over into the next. He had to develop a way of interrupting his emotions and then reset them so that he could put that moment in the past, and move on to the next thing afresh.

He couldn't take his anger, concern and sadness from the war room to the photocall with the schoolchildren. He had to reset, and then appear happy, engaged and motivated for a fun photograph with the youngsters.

When I worked in a call centre, asking for donations for a charity, there were times when the person I was calling would react angrily, and shout at me down the telephone. It could be upsetting, but I couldn't let it affect my next call. Each call had to be like the first call of the day. I had to interrupt, find the gap and reset. Each delivery, each drop, had to be done as if it was my first, my only, drop of the day.

Breathe, check my posture, start afresh.

Be here now. In this moment, and this moment only.

If you can do this in every moment of every day, then you can give any challenge your full attention. You can ensure that you are firing on all cylinders, ready to be as effective as you can be in the pursuit of the thing you are working towards. You can't be at the mercy of your emotions when you've got bigger dreams to reach for, bigger fish to fry. So you must learn to be aware of the state you are in, and develop tools and techniques to change it to the best state possible for getting stuff done. You must not only manage your time but manage yourself. Know when you are most effective at decision making, know when you might need to factor in a power nap during your working week, keep your behaviour in check so that you promote the traits you wish to see in the best version of yourself, and try to rid yourself of the behaviours that you don't wish to see. And above all you must practise kindness to yourself and others. Not punish yourself for being only human, and not judge others for the same.

To do any or all of these things you must learn to be self-aware and to live life on purpose. And at the heart of that is learning to recognise the negative thoughts within you, acknowledge them, breathe, and let go.

CHAPTER RECAP

When you run on autopilot, you often react to internal and external stimuli emotionally, and not always in your best interests. By using a variety of techniques to interrupt the input/output chain you can teach yourself to respond instead of reacting, and be more measured and graceful in the way you go about things. When you are in charge of your emotions rather than allowing them to control you, you can prevent situations or people from pushing your buttons, which causes you to give up your power.

CHAPTER 6: STOP COMPLAINING

"Beautify your inner dialogue. Beautify your inner world with love, light, and compassion. And life will be beautiful."
– Dr. Amit Ray

Living a life on purpose requires you to be self-aware in everything that you do. Being self-aware means that you understand your traits and behaviours, when you are operating at your most effective, when to interrupt thoughts and emotions that don't serve or benefit you, when to interrupt behaviours that don't serve or benefit you, and how to do the things that will transform you into the best version of yourself.

It means that you should aim to take as many of your daily activities as consciously and as mindfully as possible, and try not to operate on autopilot wherever you can. After all, it's autopilot that's kept you stuck in this rut, so it's time to switch your controls to manual. This is part of the fine art of living gracefully, and there is much satisfaction, enjoyment and power to be had doing this.

Two things that are such a great British past time that many people do them on autopilot – without even realising they are doing them – are complaining and judging. Complaining is something that people revel in, and spend a huge amount of time doing. It can act as a kind of cathartic release, while judging others has become so popular that it's spawned a whole industry of its own – that of celebrity gossip. But the problem with judging and complaining is that they are incredibly negative activities, that do nothing beneficial for you, and at worst do harm to you and others.

When you engage in a constant diet of complaining and judging you are allowing a huge amount of negativity into your daily routine. This negative energy becomes addictive, and detrimental to a positive, effective and upbeat state of mind.

But for the most part people complain so much that they don't even realise the extent to which they do it. That they are unconsciously engaging in a negative activity without even realising, and that they are doing it to such an extent, it's no wonder that they're living with such a negative outlook most of the time. What's even worse about complaining and judging is that they are easy, lazy ways to make us feel better about ourselves at the expense of others. But just like choosing the easy, lazy option of a greasy beef burger instead of making the effort to cook a wholesome healthy dinner, these negative acts can be harmful to our emotional health.

We have already talked about viewing the world with a positive perspective. But how can you realistically expect yourself to have a more upbeat outlook when you are engaged in the national pastime of moaning and being horrible about other people?

Being negative about other people and about situations, while they may be enjoyable activities to engage in at the time, will only serve to depress you even more than you already are. If you're stuck in a rut, then this behaviour will contribute to keeping you there. If you're going backwards, this kind of behaviour will send you there faster.

When you feel like life is being harsh and unkind, how can you expect anything different when you are harsh and unkind to others, about everything, all the time. But when you make an effort to change the way you view others, to embrace a much more empathic and understanding approach to life, and when you are no longer controlled by your negative emotions but much more accepting of the ups and downs of reality, then not only do you become kinder and more accepting of your brothers and sisters around the world, but your own world becomes much more accepting to you.

When you see another person, you see only a small part of their story. When you read about someone in the newspaper, when you hear about someone on the television news, you see just a fraction of reality. To make a judgement based on what little information you actually have would be foolish, so why not offer the benefit of the doubt – at worst reserving judgement, at best thinking better of them.

Before you complain about how awful something is, which for many is the initial knee-jerk reaction to almost any situation, why don't you put it in context or try to understand it with an open mind first? Was the meal really that bad? Was the waiter really that unprofessional? Or are you forgetting that the restaurant is run by humans who, just like us, are imperfect? Is that email really annoying, or is there something to learn from it? Is that person's constant stream of questions a nuisance, or an opportunity for you to help someone?

I spent three years as working as a carer for the disabled. I think 'disabled' is a terrible blanket term because some of the people I worked with were much more 'able' than me – or indeed most people I know. One was a qualified doctor, another was an entrepreneur, and some had more 'everyday' jobs like working in supermarkets or as kitchen assistants. What they all had in common, though, was that they needed help doing some of the tasks the rest of us take for granted, and they needed to be able to do those things with the dignity that anybody – disabled or not – should be afforded.

Imagine if you needed help typing because you couldn't use your hands. Imagine if you needed someone to talk on the phone for you, because you couldn't speak. Imagine being unable feed yourself, wash yourself or go to the toilet, but you were smarter than anyone you knew and your mind was as sharp as a tack. As a carer, it was my job to help other people live as normal a life as possible, with as much dignity as possible, so they could focus on rest of their daily routines without getting weighed down by the things they couldn't do – things that you and I take for granted. So that they could carry on being doctors, entrepreneurs, or working in the supermarket or the kitchen.

It would have been easy to complain about this job. It would have been easy to think that my life was awful, having to help someone else in the bathroom, or having to feed them their food. But it wasn't awful. How could

I complain about feeding someone their lunch, when I was sat opposite someone who couldn't feed themselves? How could I complain about helping someone else go to the toilet, when I was with someone who was unable to do that for themselves? Any complaint I might have made or even thought, would have immediately paled in comparison to what the person in front of me had to deal with every minute of every day. To think it would have been to dishonour and disrespect the person I was helping, and would dishonoured and disrespected the better version of myself.

I couldn't complain, so I didn't. I couldn't be late for work, so I wasn't. I couldn't have a drink in the evening, so I didn't. I couldn't hit snooze, so I didn't. I had to subjugate my own needs because the needs of the people I was working with were far, far greater. Their story was far more complex than my own. And if I were to complain and make the situation about me, it would be doing them a disservice, and it would be making my own situation one that was uncaring, and unbearable.

When we complain or judge negatively a person or a situation we multiply the negativity. Not only is the situation bad, but we are vocalising it, dwelling on how bad it is, and in doing so the stress increases, the negativity grows. But when we choose not to complain, to let go of the irritation and leave the ants to go on their way in peace, then the situation becomes bearable, we create space to consider the story of the person we're judging. And in doing so we let go of our own personal tension and resistance and our own existence becomes more calm, serene and beautiful.

As a carer, I took great satisfaction from being able to offer some sort of dignity and normality to the people I was helping, even though I could have seen the job as awful. I was a lifeline for them, a friend, someone they could turn to when they needed help getting on with life. Had I complained, I would have made my position intolerable. But worse than that, I would have made the life of the people I was there to help intolerable too – by an order of magnitude.

If you aim to be better, then you need to act a better person, and an easy way to do this is to stop complaining and to stop judging people. Two simple things, which at first are hard to do, but like everything else, with practice, will reap benefits in terms of your outlook on life. When you stop complaining about how awful everything is, things seem less awful. When you stop judging people for being so imperfect, people seem more perfect. More human. More relatable. More like you.

Have you ever had a conversation with a colleague about someone else, knowing deep down that the colleague you're chatting with is probably having that same conversation with someone else, about you? What if you were to stop indulging in that kind of chat? What if people were to know that you aren't the kind of person who chats about people behind their back? What if you maintained the integrity of not talking ill of people when they aren't present – celebrities or otherwise? How much nicer would the world appear? How much better would you feel?

If you want life to be nicer, then you need to be nicer. If you want to have less to complain about, stop complaining so much. If you want people to stop talking about you behind your back, stop talking about them behind their back. Develop your integrity. Be the person that you want other people to see you as, and you will be well on your way to developing the life you want. You will be well on the way to being the kind of person you want to be.

If you want your perspective to remain positive you must not only look out for positive things, but you must also refrain from engaging in negative behaviour. It's a small practice, but it's one that pays huge dividends. If you want to be treated fairly and kindly, you must treat others with that same kindness and fairness.

Life returns what you give to it, so give it positivity and you will receive it back. Don't judge, and don't complain, and it will have a huge benefit for your positive perspective. Engage in this practice, and you will find there is more to enjoy, more to benefit from, more opportunities to be had, more joy to be found, and more satisfaction and happiness in your life. The way we behave in life is reflected back to us.

Those who complain the most have the most to complain about. Those who judge often find themselves judged. It doesn't have to be that way, and with practice and patience, it won't be.

As the Buddhist proverb states: "Bow to the mirror, and the mirror bows back."

CHAPTER RECAP

Those who complain the most have the most to complain about. If you can stop yourself giving voice to and engaging in negative behaviours such as constantly complaining and judging other people and situations, you will view the world in a much more positive way, have a much more positive life, and you will act with integrity and kindness when dealing with others and yourself.

CHAPTER 7: WHAT ARE YOU FRIGHTENED OF?

"Our fears are always more in number than our dangers."
– Seneca the Younger

I was about to give a speech to hundreds of people. It was my first solo exhibition of photographic work in a Danish gallery and I was terrified. I felt exposed. What would people think of me? What would they think of my work? Some of the themes of the pictures dealt with serious issues, and here I was, a photographer, what did I know about serious issues? I wasn't clever enough to be talking about things with such gravity. That sort of thing is normally done by people much more intelligent, more grown-up, with more gravitas than me. My hands were shaking. I was sweating. And everyone was waiting for me to give my speech. I was frightened.

I wanted to run away, but what would everyone think of me if I did that? Whichever way I turned the options were terrifying. I was scared. But fear is a response to danger. There was no danger here. So why was I terrified?

I gave my speech to all those important people, and they clapped politely. I have no idea what they thought of me, and that's not important. But I learned that as emotional beings, one of the biggest problems we face is that we attach an emotional value to things where there really should be none. And most of the time that emotion is fear.

Fear often hides itself among other feelings, thoughts and actions, that manifest in certain behaviours and activities to the extent that we don't truly appreciate the detrimental effect that it has on our lives. It causes us to develop negative thought patterns, and it stops us from doing new things, trying new experiments and going on new adventures. It prevents us from realising our potential. Fear causes us to have unkind thoughts about others, it causes us to feel anxiety and fear, and it drains our energy and power.

Every time you hear yourself asking "but what if it doesn't work out?" or "what will people think?" or "what's the point?" or "why bother?", it's fear in the driving seat, and it's putting on the brakes.

Fear is a funny old thing though. Originally designed to protect us from rampaging woolly mammoths and sabre-toothed tigers, we face far fewer genuine dangers these days than we did thousands of years ago, so fear looks for other places where it thinks it's being helpful. But instead it's getting in the way, choking us, holding us back, promoting a negative vision of ourselves.

Speaking to large groups of people is scary, but it's not actually dangerous. Asserting yourself is scary but it's not actually dangerous. Starting a new project which seems immense in scale is scary, but it's not actually dangerous.

Wrestling a jaguar is dangerous. Climbing a mountain is dangerous. There are lots of things that are dangerous and which rightly fill us with fear. But there are other things we do every day which are much more dangerous than public speaking, or learning a new skill or asking for a pay-rise, but they don't fill us with fear at all. Riding a bicycle, crossing the road, boiling water for a cup of tea, or chopping food with a sharp knife are dangerous activities which we do every day without any kind of fear. Instead, most of the times when fear manifests itself, the danger is an illusion and we allow it to manipulate us when the actual danger level is very small – even non-existent – and we behave in irrational ways as a result.

Learning a new skill is not dangerous, but we allow fear to prevent us from starting. 215 people were killed by falling televisions in the United States between the years 2000 and 2011 – but we're not afraid of televisions. Public Speaking terrifies most people, but won't kill you, yet an estimated 3,800 people over the age of 65 are killed each year tripping over rugs. But when was the last time a rug filled you with fear? More people die choking on hotdogs every year, than die from embarrassment, but I don't know anyone who is afraid of hotdogs.

And it's not just plain old fear that's stopping us from being the best version of ourselves, and realising our dreams and achievements. Fear comes with a whole entourage of henchmen who are really just fear in a different costume.

When we get angry because we haven't got our way, or because we feel humiliated, it's fear talking and allowing our emotions to get the better of us when we should be the ones in charge, not them. When we get nervous about putting forward an idea, it's fear in the driving seat. When we don't start that new project, it's fear telling us we're going to fail, so there's really no point getting started.

Most of the time, when fear stops us from taking action, the only real risk is that we might waste some time. Imagine starting evening classes to learn a new language, but what if we don't complete the course or find time to do the homework? We'll have wasted all that time, the course fees, the effort, and it will have been for nothing. So instead we waste even more time doing nothing, rather than starting something that we may or may not complete.

Well there's a solution to that. Make the effort to see it through to the end. Master the mundane aspects of daily life and find time to do the coursework. Master yourself, develop the integrity to see it through to the end, complete the course and learn the language. No one is stopping you from achieving your goal other than you, and you're using fear to give yourself an excuse not to bother.

That's the problem with fear – it gives us an easy way out. The "what if" that stops us from doing the scary thing is just us giving ourselves an excuse to not do that thing. And the result is we stay right here, where we are, treading water, running on the treadmill. Safe and sound and cosy, because trying anything, going to the effort to improve, is scary. What if we make that effort, spend the energy, give up all that time, and it doesn't work? What will people think of us, all those people who also never try to achieve anything? It's scary, isn't it?

The problem is that new projects require discipline, success comes with responsibility, and that means you must make the effort. But as we are about to learn, the satisfaction that comes from taking life by the horns, owning the challenge and taking responsibility for the outcome, is as powerful as the success of the project itself. When we tell ourselves that we can succeed, that we are determined to do what is required to make something happen, and that we have so much ownership of our lives that we will create the space to do so, then almost anything is possible.

Fear, on the other hand, would like us to stay under the duvet. Fear likes things to be easy, safe, and doesn't like to make the effort. Fear wants us to have the easy life, the 9 to 5 that can keep us ticking over, but will never deliver anything more than the ordinary (but that's fine because ordinary is safe). But fear also makes us feel frustrated, powerless, incapable. It compares us to those other people and says that we're not good enough to have a car like that, a big house like that, a life like that. It tells us that we don't understand, that it's far too complex for us, and we'd better leave it to someone else to have the achievement, the success, the grown-up things.

But the thing is, we're not placed on this planet to make up the numbers. Our existence is not just a conveyor belt from birth to death, waiting for the inevitable while we try not to rock the boat, or cause a scene. Life is about seeing what we're capable of, what lights our fire, and shouting "who cares what anyone else thinks?"

When we find ourselves intimidated, stepping back to avoid confrontation, biting our tongue, or not speaking up, we must remember the gap that we use to interrupt the stimulus and choose our response. We must take that moment to stop our reflexive action, assess what real danger there is in doing the thing, and then go and do it. Through practice, discipline, searching for discomfort, and stepping out of our comfort zone, we can recognise our fear, listen to what it's saying, and then go and do it anyway.

When we remember that doing 'the thing' has no real danger, that doing 'the thing' will rarely result in us plunging to our deaths, being eaten by tigers or getting crushed by a falling piano, then we realise that what we perceive to be danger is a figment of our imagination. We might be scared of public speaking, but where is the danger? When we give in to the 'what ifs' we give away our power, but when we go and do 'the thing', when we step out on stage, write that book, take that risk, and we realise there is no danger, nothing to fear at all, then we gain power. We grow, we develop, and we have the chance to be extraordinary. But if we give in to fear than we can expect nothing but disappointment, nothing but boring, nothing but the same old same old. Nothing but the ordinary.

Think for a moment. What's more frightening – living a better life in ten years' time, or being exactly where you are right now in ten years' time? When was the last time an unpleasant experience actually did us any harm? It's time to stop being frightened and start taking action.

Because once you start standing up to fear, you'll feel like the bravest person in the world, and you'll know that there's nothing to fear but fear itself. Fear will keep you safe here and now, but it will also stifle you, hold you back, and keep you trapped – if you let it. So don't let it. Take back your power, and take a step towards realising your potential. There's a whole world out there, and it's yours for the taking – providing you're not too scared to grab it.

CHAPTER RECAP

Fear is an ancient emotion designed to protect cavemen from sabre-toothed tigers. But in the modern world we often experience fear when there is no real danger, and instead find ourselves prevented from taking beneficial action because we fear "what will people think?", "what if it doesn't work out?", "what if it all goes wrong?" If we can see fear for what it is – an illusion – and push past it, there's no end to what we can achieve.

CHAPTER 8: FORGIVE YOURSELF TODAY

"Do not dwell in the past, do not dream of the future, concentrate the mind on the present moment." – Buddha

We've already mentioned how our self-talk gets in the way of us achieving anything, how fear has us in a choke hold, and how our negative thought patterns serve as a reminder of how things will never work out for us. We fixate on these negative thoughts, and this fixation uses up capacity that would be better spent elsewhere. Often this self-talk is about how we're not good enough, how we know we're only going to fail so there's no point starting. We waste time, effort, energy and capacity worrying what people will think, rather than trying to be productive, sort our lives out, and learn how to 'deal with it'.

All too often we spend time and capacity mentally – and therefore emotionally – punishing ourselves for past failures, misdeeds, inadequacies and other negative things from our past that not only feed our anxiety, but also provide evidence for why we shouldn't do anything in the future. Why try anything when past evidence shows we'll only fail, or not finish it, or embarrass ourselves, or do a really bad job?

The thing is, while we exist in three time periods, we can only exert influence over two of them, and we can only take action in one of them. We should be focusing on the actions that we can take in this moment, right now, that will benefit us tomorrow, next week, next month, or in ten years' time. But instead, we worry about the things we did yesterday, last month, last year, when we were terrible teenagers.

If we intend to 'deal with it', to take ownership of our lives, and work to build a better tomorrow, we need to forgive ourselves the misdemeanours of yesterday and move on. That's not to say that we should forget the error of our ways, but if we can recognise where we went wrong in the past, we can work to be better in the future. But if we fixate on the past, without using that energy to take beneficial action to shape our future and be better in it instead, then we are wasting our time, capacity, and torturing ourselves for no good reason.

While we have no influence over the past, we can decide what influence it can have over our present, in order that we can learn what actions to take to shape our future. Indeed, if we can look back at any experience and learn from it, then nothing is a waste of time, because it is an opportunity to learn, to improve, and be better versions of ourselves.

Yet, time and time again we worry, we fixate, we stress about things that are long gone, and in doing so we not only give away our power to change our future, but we also give away our capacity to use our time in the present – in the now – effectively.

As I moved from job to job, desperately trying to find success, I felt like I was wasting time. I spent a year working in a bank, eight years as a journalist, three years as a carer for the disabled, a year as van driver, and in many cases I could feel my life slipping away, day by day, hour by hour, minute by minute. I would look back and think, if only I hadn't wasted all that time doing this job or that job, I could have been creating something significant, a body of work, a legacy, a fortune, a reputation, a wonderful life for myself.

I would beat myself up, spend hours with my mind racing about the missed opportunities, cursing myself for not studying harder at school, for not staying with this career or that career. But then I realised that no amount of mental or emotional energy could change the past, that it was done and gone, and the time was only wasted if I didn't learn anything, gain anything, or benefit from the experiences somehow. And when I looked back at my past I realised that it was a patchwork quilt of experiences, a cornucopia of jobs, activities, things I'd done, things I'd experienced, and I finally knew I could learn from them all.

The things we are ashamed of, where we have disappointed ourselves – if we can forgive ourselves and learn from them, we can become better people by taking action right now to influence our future. And in doing so, start to build a new, more positive past that won't haunt us, but will instead fill us with pride and a sense of accomplishment each time we look back.

Those jobs I'd taken when I needed the money, they all had something to teach me about the world, about myself, and those teachings could be put to use right now, with action that would make me a better person tomorrow, that would shape my life in the years to come. All that time I'd wasted in seemingly dead-end existences wasn't wasted at all, as long as I could put it to good use in shaping my future. When we stop punishing ourselves for our pasts, and instead learn from them, then no experience is a waste of time, and everything has something to help us improve, become better, shape our realities.

Whether it was learning how to slice cheese when I worked as a kitchen hand one summer, or when I burned out as a magazine editor and got a job in a warehouse smashing up computers for six months, or when I attended an awards dinner at the Guggenheim Museum in New York, or when I delivered the weekly shop to an old lady at the top of a block of flats at the seaside, I've learned something every step of the way. And rather than dwell on those wasted hours, days, months and years, I've managed to forgive myself and take what I've learned to propel myself forward. And you can too.

Those things that you punish yourself for, those things you're ashamed of, the wasted opportunities, those crimes against humility, the fashion mistakes, the blooper reels, the faux pas, the failed attempts at comedy, the poor exam results, the times you were too mean, too meek, too mild, the times you were offensive, when you upset people, when you upset yourself, when you fell off your bicycle, when you stubbed your toe, when you let yourself go, when you looked in the mirror and cried. All those things that constantly buzz around your head when you've got nothing else to focus your mind on, those things that keep you hiding under the duvet instead of getting out and changing the world, those thoughts that won't leave you alone. Take ownership of them. Claim them as yours. Forgive yourself and learn from them. And let go of them so that you can get on with your future.

All these things can be used as source material for doing better next time. All these things can be used as lessons to make you wise, make you stronger and better. Every time you failed is one more step to becoming the best version of yourself.

There isn't a self-help book in the world that doesn't feature Thomas Edison and his quest to create the lightbulb, but that's because it's a great metaphor for this idea of learning from your past. It took Edison more than ten thousand attempts before he came up with the working prototype for the electric lightbulb. He could have chosen to see himself as a multiple-failure and let that define him, or he could learn from each of those failures and use them as a step towards success. By refusing to let his past defeat him, but learning from it and moving forward, he didn't just find success but he changed the world in the process. As Edison famously said: "I've not failed. I've just found 10,000 ways that won't work."

When we become paralysed by our pasts, when we punish ourselves repeatedly for our mistakes, our wasted efforts and time, when instead we can be looking for the learning in all of them, we do a disservice to ourselves, to our future, and the action we could be taking right now.

We owe it to ourselves to work to be the best we can

be, to realise as much of our potential as possible, and to use the power we have – the power we can choose to nurture for ourselves every day of our lives – to create the best possible life for ourselves. But when we spend our time and capacity punishing ourselves, we short change our future.

So, next time you find yourself obsessing about that thing from yesterday, that error of judgement from a month ago, that missed opportunity from a year ago, or that embarrassing moment from your childhood, recognise it as negative self-talk, and interrupt it. Remember, you only give energy to the thoughts that serve you, and if these thoughts aren't serving you, put your mind to work on something much more beneficial. Something that doesn't lead to negative emotions, but empowers you to face the day ahead and make the most of it. There's work to be done today to build a better tomorrow, and it won't get done by obsessing about the past.

Use your power to move forward, to extract the learning, growth and wisdom from every experience, and use that to become the best version of yourself. Understand your flaws, build your self-awareness, become wise and stoic, but forgive yourself. You're not perfect, but you are human, and in those imperfections lies your beauty, your greatness and the opportunity to be the person you always dreamed of being. Learn, grow, move forward.

Forgiving yourself gives you an opportunity to uncover and recognise your power, and that power can come from discovering your limits, your weaknesses, your chances to improve, the opportunities to know yourself better. Forgive yourself right now, change your thinking, and direct your thoughts forward instead of back. You can't change the past, but you can change the future, and that's vital if you're ever going to learn to 'deal with it'.

At the heart of self-forgiveness is gentle kindness, the type of kindness that we should be showing to everyone around us, but which we often forget to show to ourselves. We are human, we are fallible, we make mistakes, take wrong turns, go down dead ends. But with each wrong turn comes an opportunity to take the right turn next time, to improve, to learn. Just like Thomas Edison.

When we constantly punish ourselves, and live in that perpetual state of self-doubt, unable to see the future because we are obsessing about the past, then we are not only standing still and stagnating but we are moving backwards in very real terms. Life goes on with or without us, like a river moving constantly from source to sea. You can't dive in and swim with the current if you're standing looking backwards. And if you're standing looking backwards, you'll get washed away.

So be kind to yourself. Recognise your failures. Understand where you went wrong. Acknowledge it, learn from it, be stronger, be better, be kinder and let your power grow. You are human, and you've got important work to do. All this time worrying about the past won't help you build your future, so stop focusing on your weakness and find your superpowers.

CHAPTER RECAP

We cannot change the past, but we can change the future, by taking action in the present. But we can't take beneficial action if our time and capacity is being used up in the futile activity of worrying about past events. Better to forgive yourself, acknowledge the past, learn from it, and use that learning to grow and be better in the future.

CHAPTER 9: YOU'RE ALREADY A SUPERHERO

"The sun shines not on us, but in us." – John Muir

I had been applying for jobs for over a year. Every day the job alerts would flow into my inbox faster than I could read them. Job after job, vacancy after vacancy, and I would spend all my spare time going over them, sending off my CV (or résumé if you're American) for roles that I thought I could do, that I thought would be bearable to turn up to every day, week after week. If I was lucky I would get a rejection letter. Usually I wouldn't get any response.

I'd been using the same CV my entire career. When I left a job I would add a new section to the top of the document outlining my previous role, and then as the job alerts filled my inbox I would send the latest version of my CV off. Time and time again, feeling lucky if I heard anything back at all.

But the result of all this effort, which at best earned me a rejection, was that I felt useless. I felt as if I had nothing to offer. Nobody wanted to hire me. I had wasted years of my life, and now I was worthless. Unhireable. Unemployable. Unwanted. My self-worth was at an all-time low. After all I'd been through, after all the years of hard work, I wasn't worth anything, to anyone.

I realised that my CV, the same CV that I had been using for all these years, wasn't working for me. And if something doesn't work then you should try something different. Rewriting it was a boring, arduous task, but as Emerson said, "do the thing, and you will have the power." So I did the thing, I created a new blank document and set about rewriting my résumé.

When we look at other people, we often see their strengths first. We see how beautiful they are or how strong and tall they are. We see the fancy clothes they wear. And then we see their skills. How far they've come, the car the drive, the holidays they go on, and the smiles on their faces.

When we look at ourselves, we see the times we've failed. We see the debt we've accrued, the times we've been rejected, the failed relationships, the embarrassing moments, the days we've wasted feeling sorry for ourselves, unable to leave the house because there's nothing out there for us.

We compare ourselves to others. We put on a brave face that hides our lack of self-worth. Our smile hides the fact we don't value ourselves because we have nothing to offer. But when we go out in public we feel the need to hide it, otherwise everyone will know what a failure we are. What we don't realise is that everyone else's smiles hide the same thing. Their nice clothes, perfect hair and winning lives are a veneer that covers anxiety, a whole life of experiences good and bad, and their own distorted perspective.

When life merely happens to you, when you are unable

to own it, to take control, to 'deal with it' on the most basic level, you fixate on the negative. At the beginning of the book I talked about our filters, how our perception affects the way we interact with the world, and it had been pointed out to me that whenever I talked about my achievements, I would always add a negative caveat to the end of the sentence. I would say something like "I did this thing, but it wasn't very good" or "I've also done something like that, but the one someone else did was better". I would always play down my achievement and, as the saying goes, "hide my light under a bushel". I was doing myself an injustice because, in a way, I was embarrassed of having achieved something of value. Strangely, I took comfort in the humility of failure, and struggled with how to present my successes.

So I set myself a task of removing my subjective emotions from the activity of writing my CV, and began noting my accomplishments and achievements in an objective way. As I began to list the things I'm good at, the things I'd achieved, this simple, boring activity became a really positive, confidence-boosting exercise that began to transform how I saw myself. No caveats. I highly recommend it.

You see, when you're trying to sell a car you don't advertise the flat tyre, the high mileage, or that strange clanking sound it makes when you turn a corner. But when we are advertising ourselves far too often we fixate on our faults and weaknesses, when a simple change in perspective is all it takes to realise that, actually, we're not completely worthless. And, actually, we might have more to offer than we realise.

And so I want to share with you the exercise that I undertook to help me rewrite my CV, and which ultimately helped me rewrite my self-worth. Grab your notebook – the positivity book that you've been writing the things you're grateful for and all the positive experiences in – and do what I did.

Turn to a new double page. At the top of the left-hand page write "STRENGTHS," and on the right-hand page write "WEAKNESSES". These are your headings, and give you an idea of what I want you to do next. However, I want you to draw a line through the right-hand page. You're not allowed to write anything on this page. This notebook is, after all, a totem of positivity, so while you're doing this exercise every time you think of a reason that you're not good enough, a flaw, something you're not very good at, something you've failed at, I want you to acknowledge it, but then let it go and move on straight away.

You're only going to write on the left-hand page. This exercise is about writing down your achievements, the things you've done, the accomplishments, the things you're good at, that you're proud of, that highlight the very best of you. You must do this truthfully. And you can't stop until the page is full.

Start with your high school qualifications. If you find yourself thinking "but my grade in that subject wasn't very good" acknowledge that thought, and move on. Stay positive. If you went to college, list those qualifications too. Every time a thought pops into your head that starts with "but…" acknowledge it and move on.

What about your achievements? Your skills? You have some, whether you believe it or not, and when you find your thoughts leaning towards the negative, towards the page with the header "WEAKNESSES" stop yourself, and bring your thoughts back to the left-hand page. The page with "STRENGTHS" at the top.

Breathe. Adjust your posture. Move on.

If, like me, you thought of yourself as worthless, with nothing to offer, you'll find this exercise difficult at first. But keep going, because once the floodgates open, you'll find it hard to stop.

On my STRENGTHS page, I listed all my qualifications – it didn't matter what the grade was, if I earned a qualification I listed it. I'm qualified journalist. I wrote that down. I had run a marathon, so I wrote "marathon runner" on that left-hand page. Many years previously I'd had a book about web design published, so I wrote down "published author". I had worked in New York editing a magazine, so I wrote down "international magazine editor". I had made videos just for fun and for a previous job, so I wrote "videographer". I was a podcaster, a professional photographer, I was good at image retouching, I had commissioned writers, photographers, illustrators. It all went down on that left-hand page.

But this exercise was no longer about creating a new CV. Just like selling a car, I was focusing on all my best bits, and you should too. Each time I found myself thinking of a weakness, I would look at the line I had drawn through the right-hand page, and bring my mind back to the STRENGTHS page. I wrote down "funny", "compassionate", "kind", "clever". I was good at cooking, so I wrote that down too. I was organised, thoughtful, productive. It all went down on that left-hand page.

Before long the page was full of positive words that made me special, more than ordinary. But I couldn't stop. I filled the margins, wrote in all the gaps, words and phrases that outlined my skills, accomplishments, things I was proud of.

On more than one occasion I had been required to speak to large groups of people, and although it was an activity that terrified me, I wrote down "public speaker". I had been to lots of countries around the world so I wrote down "world traveller". I once won an award for something so I wrote "award winner". Every time I thought to myself "that doesn't really count because…" I acknowledged that thought, discarded it and moved on.

All these things were true. No embellishments, no falsehoods. I was writing down all my best bits. Looking over the list I realised that I had already been pushing my limits my entire life. I realised that I had achieved lots of things that compound a little bit at a time. When I looked at that list I knew that I was beyond ordinary. I was extraordinary.

At first this exercise was difficult for me. But the more I did it the easier it became to find positive things about myself. It reminded me of the short period of time during my childhood when I was in the Cub Scouts. To encourage us to be wholesome young men and to develop strong morals, we were set a task. Every week we had to do daily good deeds, and write them down in a notebook. At each weekly Cub Scout meeting we would present our list of weekly good deeds to the scout leader, and each week those who had done the most deeds would receive a badge.

Each week I would see the other Cubs getting new badges to sew on to their uniforms, but each week I returned with an empty notebook. I hadn't managed to find any good deeds to do and I felt like a bad person, with bad morals. I didn't last long at Cubs, and when I finally decided enough was enough, I left without ever receiving a single badge.

It was only later that I learned that all the things that the other Cubs were writing in their notebooks, were all the things that I took for granted. I had been doing good deeds every day without even thinking about it. I didn't need to be asked to do them, I just thought that was the right way to behave. I hadn't needed encouragement or a reward to have good morals, I just did them anyway, and thought that was normal behaviour. And while all the other Cubs were announcing their good deeds and I thought myself a bad person, I was simply taking for granted the good deeds that other people had to make an effort to remind themselves do.

The point is, it's easy to overlook things that we may not even consider to be positive values, but which other people might consider worthy of celebration. So really take a good look at your life, the things you do, the things you've taken for granted. Write your list. Put down all the things you've done. Be honest, but don't hide your light under a bushel. Be objective about all the things you're good at. Are you a strong swimmer? Are you caring? Do you speak a second language? Are you a persistent person who will see a project through to the end? Are you persuasive? Are you a stamp collector? Are you good at drawing? Are you a good typist? Do you really listen when others need to talk? What are your interests? What lights your fire?

Write your list until all the space on the page is full. Write it until you've forgotten all the 'buts'. Write it until you understand that you're not worthless, that you're not ordinary, that you have vast amounts to offer the world. And then recognise that this is you. You are all these things. You are extraordinary.

These are your superpowers. You're already a superhero.

This exercise should be enough to show you that you are already far better, far more accomplished, more capable, with more to offer than you previously thought. This exercise should be enough to change your perspective of yourself. Remove the negative emotions that warp your perspective of yourself and objectively understand that you are amazing.

How much do you think you're worth now? How much are you capable of? How does a person who can do what you do, who has your skills, experience and abilities act? How do they carry themselves? How do they go about getting stuff done? Because that person who does all that, who has all those things to offer the world, is you. Isn't it time you started behaving like that?

And knowing now what you've achieved, what you're good at, what your superpowers are, look forward. With all these powers in your armoury, what else could you achieve? How far can you go if you were only to take action, if you were only to start something, if you could only organise the rest of your day in order to make space for your next achievement?

Now go and do it.

CHAPTER RECAP

When you remove emotion from the equation, and truly, objectively look at your achievements, skills and experiences, you'll be surprised at just how amazing you really are. Make an honest list without bragging or hiding your light under a bushel, and you'll realise you're extraordinary. You're already a superhero.

PART 2: RETAIN YOUR POWER

CHAPTER 10: DON'T GIVE IT AWAY

"You have power over your mind – not outside events. Realise this, and you will find strength." – Marcus Aurelius

In the introduction I described that this book is split into three sections, each of which outline the three steps to learning how to 'deal with it.'

Find your power.
Retain your power.
Grow your power.

As I explained, your 'power' is shorthand for all the positive stuff about you, all the achievements, the strength, the ability to take beneficial action, and those actions themselves. It is your integrity, your self-esteem and your self-confidence. In the first section, we looked at how to dig it out from underneath years of negative programming and thought patterns, and in this short section we're going to look at how you can avoid giving your power away. All this talk of power is inspired by the Ralph Waldo Emerson quote that gives this book its title: "Do the thing, and you will have the power."

In the first section of the book we were like explorers in the jungle, cutting back vines that blocked our path, and we talked about cutting back all the negativity, the bad self-talk and the anxiety that holds us back and stops us from realising our true worth and our potential to improve ourselves and our lives. We learned that if we can interrupt negative patterns of thought, emotion and behaviour we can free up capacity to do much better things instead, and we learned how our mind belongs to us, how it is a potent tool for creativity, but it is not us. And every time we allow our self-talk to sabotage us it's like being slapped across the face by our own hand.

Now we're moving on to the second part of our journey, which is all about retaining our power. Our power is only useful to us if we can hold on to it, and stop it being buried again under the negative thinking which will take us back to square one. This section of the book is about being mindful of those influences that would seek to undermine us, whether they come from within us or from outside us.

If you're like me, then you can be sensitive to comments from other people, and all it takes is one word and you can find yourself doubting your actions and your decision making. That is a perfect example of giving your power away. Another is when we allow other people or situations to 'push our buttons', causing us to react emotionally when we'd be much better off pausing and responding in a measured, graceful way.

Similarly, we give up power to organisations, devices, drama and individuals who want us to feel outraged, sad, or guilty or just want to take up all our time and attention, which would be better used elsewhere more beneficially. We allow ourselves to be manipulated by news sources, by marketing and advertising, by fashions and trends. But when we learn that information always comes to us twice, then we can see what's happening, hold on to our power and not be manipulated.

First there's the information itself, and second is the agenda with which it is given to you. What response is the person or organisation delivering the information trying to elicit from you? Are they trying to make you angry, to make you buy something, support their political party, think ill of someone else, to get you to support their cause, use their product, become hooked on their device? Think of it as a transaction – you think the information is free, but in truth you're expected to pay something for it.

When we become aware of our environment, the forces at work within it, their agenda, and all the things around us that are vying for our attention, our capacity, our emotional response and our power, we are much better placed to be able to retain it, and disempower those who would seek to manipulate us.

A lot of the time those who seek to manipulate us don't even know they're doing it, but when we can step back, disentangle ourselves emotionally, and adopt a stoic approach to any situation, then we are much more able to 'deal with it'. A crisis is much easier to tackle if we can approach it calmly and logically. It's much easier to see through political propaganda if we can understand the intent with which it is served. It is much easier to withdraw from the manipulation of the news organisations when we are aware of their intent, their politics, and their aims.

When we can retain our power, it grows. While the

third section of the book is all about using and growing our power, every time we so much as recognise the power within us, or that we have successfully held on to it when we could have given it away, it grows stronger. When we find our power, our power grows. When we retain our power, it grows. Our power feeds itself every time it is seen and appreciated and used in a positive, beneficial way.

You've already experienced this when you used your power to interrupt your negative thought patterns. That, in itself, is empowering. You may have even found yourself asking "if I can use my power to change my way of thinking, what else can I use it for? What else can I achieve?"

When you react automatically to any stimulus, you give your power away. When you allow the agenda with which information is served to you to influence your reaction, you are giving your power away. When you allow a media source to manipulate your emotions, you are giving your power away. But when you respond in a conscious, measured way, you retain your power and it grows. Living life gracefully and on purpose retains and grows your power. Taking beneficial actions retains and grows your power. Recognising when something or someone is trying to manipulate you and 'push your buttons' and refusing to allow it, grows your power and moves you forward. And moving forward is fundamental to owning life, and living gracefully.

Standing still, on the other hand, is the same as moving backwards. It causes stagnation, loss of momentum, and doesn't serve to either retain or grow your power.

Constant conscious forward movement is always required, and that's what this book aims to impart. Keep improving, guard your power, and be aware of those forces that would see it taken from you. The more you give your power away, the more you can be manipulated, the more likely you are to act and react in ways that don't represent the best version of you, and the more your positive energy will give way to negative energy.

And before you know it, where you were once able to 'deal with it', suddenly you may find you cannot. This book is all about taking ownership of your life, of learning how to deal with it, and go from being trapped by the ordinary to being its master and becoming extraordinary. And the only way to do that is to hold on to your power, nurture it, and use it to make yourself better every day, in every way.

CHAPTER 11: WHOSE MIND IS IT ANYWAY?

"Emancipate yourselves from mental slavery. None but ourselves can free our minds." – Bob Marley

I was sinking. I had been sinking for a long time. And everywhere I turned there were more pebbles to fill up my pockets and make me sink further, faster, into darker depths.

My inbox was full of desperate pleas for help. Charities, all of whom I shared a moral value structure with, all needed my help. Lots of them. Each day another email would appear begging for support. Pleading for money to feed the starving, end cruelty, fight injustice, save the planet. But I couldn't help myself, let alone help them. I felt guilty. Powerless.

Every time I turned on the news there was another tragedy that I was unable to help with. Another political crisis that I needed to be angry about, but could do nothing to change. Every advertising hoarding told me I wasn't good enough, cool enough, glamorous enough, that my kitchen surface was covered in deadly germs, that all my teeth were about to fall out, that I was unhealthy and going to die.

My mind was awash with guilt, fear, anger, sorrow, sadness, and all of it topped off with powerlessness. There was nothing I could do to change anything, and it was all my fault. The world was falling apart. I was falling apart. If only I could send a donation, buy those trainers, vote for this party, sign that petition, drive that car, drink that beer, eat at that restaurant, own those clothes, have that hairstyle, that laptop, that look, that life.

But I couldn't have those things, do those things, be those things. I couldn't save those people. I couldn't save the planet. So I did the only thing I could do.

I unsubscribed.

I unsubscribed from all the emails that tugged at my heart strings. I stopped reading all the news stories that made me angry, sad, and guilty. I stopped paying attention to advertising. And my mind and my conscience cleared. I had regained my power, and I finally I was able to see the forest where before I could only see trees. I had let go.

We've already talked about how our minds are tools for our own use, just like our arms and our legs. When we have ownership of our minds – when we employ mindfulness techniques in order to be able to step aside from our thoughts and observe them objectively, and then put our minds to use for our own needs – then they are incredibly powerful tools and we can do almost anything with them.

Think about it – mankind put people on the moon using the power of their minds. Watson and Crick discovered DNA using the power of their minds. I made a cup of coffee this morning using the power of my mind. Think about that. Then step aside and observe yourself thinking about it.

The problem occurs when we stop using our minds objectively and with intent, and instead operate on autopilot. We give up responsibility for what we're doing with our days, hours and minutes, and we hand it over to our automatic actions – to our autopilot – and to our unchecked thoughts. When we're not actively engaged with our minds – most often when we're treading water in life – that's when the negative thought processes start to take hold, when we start to feel like we are not in control of our lives. That's when we feel powerless.

In some cases, these negative thought processes have taken over control of our thinking thanks to a lifetime of negative programming. In other cases, we've been undermined, perhaps by bullies, perhaps by past failures, but in all cases we've given away our power by giving away a share in our mind's capacity. That portion of our mind's capacity could be put to much better use, but instead we've switched on the autopilot, and now our negative thought patterns and emotions are doing the driving, while we sit in the backseat looking forlorn with no influence over the direction we're going.

But it's not just negative thought processes that will take up a share of our mind's capacity (or mindshare) if we let them. We are constantly surrounded by forces and information that want some of our mindshare, and too frequently we hand it over without objectively observing what we're doing. And most of the time, as we've already observed, it's because that information comes twice.

What I mean by this is simple. While we think we are receiving a single piece of information, we are actually receiving two. The first is what we see on the surface, and the second is hidden underneath. The first is the actual information itself. You could think of this as raw data. The second is the agenda with which it's delivered. And the whole time, we're giving it our mindshare.

Take the newspapers, for example. If newspapers simply reported the truth of the news, we would only ever need one newspaper. There wouldn't be any need for others because we would have received all the facts and that would be the end of it. But instead we have lots of newspapers, and all of them have a different agenda. There are right wing newspapers and left wing newspapers. There are tabloid newspapers and broadsheets. There's serious news, and there's light news. All of it is news seen through the bias of the editors of that particular newspaper. It is information twice.

When a newspaper offers us a piece of information it's mission isn't simply to inform, but also to provoke a reaction. It might be to enrage, it might be to sadden, it might be to provoke a sense of ridicule, or it might be to encourage us to align our values with theirs. And when we react we generally believe that we have come to that reaction all on our own, that we have digested the information, and that our reaction is entirely of our own making.

In fact, we are being manipulated and controlled. We

are being told what to think and we are thinking that way because it's easier than actually thinking for ourselves, which takes effort. We are reacting instead of responding. And when we are manipulated like that, it's because we have given away mindshare to the manipulating force. We have given away our power.

Take, for example, those people who find themselves enraged by the thought of same sex marriages, by the idea of gender equality, by the concept of a black president of the United States of America, by the thought of a female president of the United States of America, by the idea of open borders or compassion for our brothers and sisters around the world. These issues are trivial things, so small in comparison to much bigger, more important issues – space exploration, curing cancer, world peace etc. – that they shouldn't even warrant questioning. If every man, woman and child were to hold on to their power and focus it on really important ideas, like ending famine, exploring other galaxies, and opening our arms and welcoming the members of our global family who all live under the same sky, there would be no limit to what mankind could achieve.

But instead we are manipulated by the twice arriving information (information + agenda) of others, hand over our mindshare, and waste our energy in narrow mindedness, indifference, heartlessness and bigotry. When we could be using our minds to bring abundance into our lives and the lives of others, we instead let others do the thinking for us, and waste our power in increasingly negative ways.

But it's not just news where this occurs. Ever find yourself laughing at the funny speaking dog in the commercial? Ever find yourself wondering how much better your life would be if you had the new smart phone from your favourite tech company? Ever find yourself worrying about the cleanliness of your kitchen because you don't have that new surface spray that kills all known germs? Ever wonder if your mindshare is being taken up by advertising? Ever wonder if you could be thinking about something much more beneficial instead?

Advertisers want our mindshare. They want us to give up our power to them. They want us to forget that they're trying to sell us something, trying to extract our money from us, and instead they want us to buy into the lifestyle, the cool, the credibility, the security of their products. And that means everything from your MP3 player to your television to your life insurance. These are all products, and when we convince ourselves that the advertiser's message is the correct one, we have given away our mindshare. We have given away our power.

But just as mindfulness teaches us to step aside from our thoughts and look at them from a more objective position (as we explored in the first section of this book) we can do the same with the external forces around us, and start to see the information and the agenda separately. When we read a newspaper and come across an article designed to enrage us, we can take a step back and absorb the information as it is, and choose not to have the emotional response. We can ask "why is this information being presented to me, what are the goals of its author, what is their agenda?"

When we see the beautifully designed advertisement for the new laptop, the new car, the clothing brand, or the food and the drink that will make us look good, that will assert ourselves as successful people, that will make us popular or confident, don't forget the agenda of the marketing people behind it. They're not presenting a piece of work for your entertainment or wonder, they're nudging you, leading you, whispering in your ear, telling you to hand over your money. Advertisements want a share of your attention and thought. They want a slice of your mindshare. They want you to prioritise what they're selling above your own free thought. They want you to hand over some of your power and when you do, they have power over you.

Advertisements are not entertainment.

I had moved to a house in North London that didn't have a television aerial. The only way I could watch TV was over the broadband connection, using streaming services. I was watching everything on catch-up and, as well as watching a lot less TV, I had also inadvertently filtered out television commercials in the process.

It wasn't apparent to me what a big deal this was until I would visit friends or family who still enjoyed their television viewing the normal way. So much of the conversation was around this television show, that advertisement, this latest news story. So much collective cultural mindshare was taken up with advertisements. So much collective emotional mindshare was being manipulated by the news. So little independent thinking was taking place because it was easier to tune in, zone out, and think what we're told to think.

It's so easy to give up our power to those entities which will take away some of the hard work, and make things easier for us. When information comes to us twice, already digested by the author's agenda, so that we can move straight on to the emotional reaction without having to interpret it for ourselves by thinking, then all the power sits with the manipulator.

When we give up our mindshare to other entities because we're too lazy to digest information for ourselves, we are allowing our perspective of the world to be controlled and manipulated by someone else. Do you see the world through your own eyes, or do you see it through the eyes of the newspaper you read or the people you hang around with? Do you believe what you're told or do you decide for yourself? Did you buy that iPhone because it's the best phone in your price range, or because Steve Jobs told you it was great? What about your politics? What about your taste in food? In holiday destination? In fashion?

It's easy to spot people who have handed over their mindshare – their capacity – and therefore their perspective to someone else, because of the language they use. Ever heard someone say the phrase "this country's full" when they talk about immigration? The country isn't full, but readers of a certain newspaper – in Britain it's the right-wing tabloid The Daily Mail, but you probably have a similar publication in your country – will all start to use the same terminology because it's what they've been told to think. What about the phrases "fake news", "shoulder to shoulder", "make no mistake", "crooked Hilary"? Phrases used by manipulators who wish to control our thinking and therefore our perspective. In the recent UK election the Conservative party intentionally repeated the phrase "strong and stable leadership" whenever they were on television, in the press or through their own literature. The idea was that if they repeated it enough they would become the party that was known to be strong and stable.

Strong and stable. Strong and stable. Strong and stable. Before long, people were voting for the Conservatives, and the reason? Because they thought they were stronger and more stable than the other parties. Whether or not that was actually true is not the point, but voters were led to believe it.

If you can shout loudest and longest, and resonate with a subject that the newspapers tell people is important, you can control the thinking of people who are too lazy to think for themselves. It's how politicians win votes, it's how Hitler won over the hearts and minds of the German people. It's how media outlets control public opinion. It's how advertisers make us fall in love with their products. It's how social media works.

Think about your own beliefs for a moment. The things that make you angry. The things that trigger emotional or impassioned responses when you read about them online or in the papers, when you see them mentioned on twitter, or reported on the television news. It might be political, it might be social, or it might be cultural. It could be anything. But think about the way those issues make you feel – do you feel that way because it's your own response, or do you feel that way because you're reacting and that's how someone else wants you to feel? How much of your perspective is yours, and how much is being manipulated by others?

How about your self-image? Could your view of yourself be manipulated by others? It's one thing for advertisers to make you feel that you'll never be cool enough, sexy enough, powerful enough unless you bankrupt yourself buying their products. But what if you're allowing others to poison not just your self-worth, but your entire perspective of yourself?

My boss was a sociopath. I was working in a creative agency just outside London, and I was always wrong. Even when I was right, I was wrong. Every day I would get berated about something that I'd done wrong, even though I knew that I had done it correctly. She would move the goalposts constantly to make life awful for me and my colleagues. She thought that was how work worked. She thought that was what it was to be a manager, and sadly that's how many managers operate. But all it did was make people miserable. Everybody feared her. Even her boss, and her boss' boss. She had the entire company in a choke-hold.

Every decision anybody made was wrong. So we stopped making decisions. And then she would be angry because she was the only person making any decisions. She was playing a game with us and we were damned if we did, and damned if we didn't.

One day one of my colleagues, someone much braver

than me, called her out on her terrible behaviour. And my boss took her apart piece by piece. My colleague left shortly after that. She took her power back, and has since gone on to do amazing things. Great things.

When you are told that you're no good repeatedly, it wears you down. It fills up your capacity. You are unable to see the positive in yourself or your life. You lose your power, and you become powerless to do anything about it. You start to believe it. You allow your perspective to be manipulated because you feel like you can't fight it any longer, and you start to think that maybe this is all there is. Maybe you are no good.

I would stay up until 4am because the thought of getting up to go to work filled me with utter dread. And so each morning I would be exhausted, with only a couple of hours' sleep, on the train to the office drinking as much coffee as I could to stay awake. And the whole journey would be spent wondering what horrors my sociopathic boss would inflict on me today. What unpleasant experiences awaited. I started to associate the taste of coffee with the taste of anxiety, and for a long time afterward I couldn't drink coffee. Like one of Pavlov's dogs, coffee made me anxious.

One night I was in a 24-hour supermarket. It was really late and I didn't need to buy anything, but it was either that or go to bed. I didn't want to go to bed because that would have meant getting up for work.

As I walked the aisles like a miserable, exhausted zombie, my tired gaze fell upon the painkillers. I found myself musing about which type would be the least painful way to go. Whichever type I went with, it seemed like a much better option than having to deal with my boss any more. Anything at all seemed better than the constant abuse, the constant character assassination, the constant bullying and undermining that was her 'style' of leadership. How many pills would I have to swallow so that I didn't have to go back to that place and face her tomorrow?

In that moment, I snapped out of it and realised where I was and what I was thinking. My capacity had been used up by this terrible person, who had undermined me and distorted my self-image so much that I no longer had any value in myself or my life. I felt worthless. I felt powerless. I felt like I had nothing to offer the world, and no reason to carry on.

But in that moment, that vivid waking moment, something changed.

I quit that job. I didn't have another job waiting, but it didn't matter. It would have been better to be completely broke and starving than to let this terrible person continue to drain my power. I quit, and in that moment I took my power back. She couldn't hurt me anymore.

We spend our lives surrounded by influences that would manipulate us, try to steal our attention, enforce their agenda upon us, and use up our capacity by causing us to doubt ourselves, devalue and undermine ourselves, distort our perspective of the world and our place in it. It takes capacity, effort and energy to create our own thoughts, to create our own identities, to choose our own path, so it's easier to let someone else do the thinking for us. Sometimes, we even have to fight to do our own thinking. But when we give our power away, when we let others control and manipulate us, we are giving away our ability to see the good within ourselves, to recognise our real strength and what we're capable of, and to realise our full potential.

So, stop for a moment, and ask yourself – who controls my thinking? Who am I giving my power to? Is it me, or is it the newspapers I read? Is it my boss who's trying to manipulate me? Is it the people I'm trying to impress, the people I'm trying to emulate, the people who are bullying me, the people whose approval I seek? Is my capacity being used up by the agendas of those who are try to sell me things, trying to part me from my money, from my own free will? Are my thoughts and emotions being manipulated by another?

Do I have full ownership of my entire being?

And if you don't, are you comfortable with that?

Let's take that capacity, that power, back.

When we refuse to be manipulated, when we recognise the agenda with which the information is presented to us, then we are able to view it as part of a bigger jigsaw and we are more empowered to put the pieces together for ourselves.

Or not.

It's up to us.

When we choose to unsubscribe from those who are vying for a piece of our mindshare, for our emotional and mental capacity, we regain that capacity for ourselves. When we refuse to be manipulated then we retain the power to make choices and decisions for ourselves, and not be lead to choices and decisions already made for us. We gain the chance to see things through our own filters, not the filters of others, and if we choose to do the work and take responsibility for our own thinking and our own world view, then there's nothing we can't do. Our mind is a powerful tool for our own use alone. It is not a resource for others.

CHAPTER RECAP

Outside entities such as news, advertising and the people around us are vying for a share of our mental and emotional capacity. They present us with information twice – the information itself and the agenda with which it is given. When we give up our mindshare we act and think in the way they command us: we buy their goods or we become enraged at their news, we see the world and ourselves with perspective they prescribe to us, not with a perspective of our own.

When we refuse to react and hand over our mindshare to others and instead retain our power and decide for ourselves how to respond, we can choose to buy the product, or get angry at the news, or we can choose not to. The power of choice and the freedom of thought are entirely ours, if we choose the responsibility and the hard work of thinking for ourselves, rather than letting someone else do it for us.

CHAPTER 12: REACTION vs. RESPONSE

"It's not stress that kills us, it is our reaction to it."
– Hans Selye

A colleague of mine was being bullied by someone at his sports club. This person would needle him, insult him, ridicule him and embarrass him in front of his friends and other people. No matter how he reacted, the bullying just got worse. The more he reacted, the more of his power he gave away, and the more powerful the bully became. The bullying just got worse.

Until one day my colleague decided not to react at all. He made a decision to respond instead, and his response was to do nothing. And then next day when faced with the bully's actions again, he chose to respond in the same way. He retained his power by choosing a response, instead of giving his power away through a reflexive reaction, and his chosen response was to do nothing. He chose not to allow the bully to 'push his buttons'.

The longer this went on, the less powerful the bully became. As my colleague refused give his power away, the bully became disempowered, until eventually he lost interest altogether and the bullying stopped.

We've already talked about choosing an intentional response instead of an automatic reaction, but it's important so it's worth mentioning again. We talked about using interruption techniques between input and output, and about how a life lived on purpose is one where your actions are carried out with thoughtful intent. But more than this, when we react to situations automatically, reflexively, we aren't just acting without thought or intent, we are giving away our power. This weakens us, begins to undo the hard work that we've put in to finding our power and tackling our negative thoughts and insecurities. It sends us backwards.

Reaction can be an emotional thing, a behavioural thing, it can be something internal, or it can be something that manifests itself for the whole world to see. But whenever we react it is rarely beneficial, and rarely graceful.

When we get angry, we are usually giving away our power. When we beep our horn or shout at another driver in traffic, we are giving away our power. When we act in an unbecoming way, we are giving away our power. When we allow our feathers to be ruffled, our hackles to rise, and allow ourselves to become irked, we are giving our power away.

But when we decide to respond, and decide upon a response that is dignified, intentional and graceful, we not only retain our power but it grows as a result. When we respond to a tense situation calmly, when we respond to a bully who feeds off our reactions by not responding at all, when we respond to blessings with gratitude, when we respond to a failure as if it's an opportunity, then we are able to shape circumstances to our will. And in doing so we can choose the best outcome possible by using all our available faculties as tools, rather than falling back to autopilot and letting our emotions do the driving.

How we do this comes back to mindfulness. In the same way that meditation and mindfulness are about acknowledging our thoughts while stepping aside from them, choosing a response instead of a reaction comes down to being able to step aside from any given situation, acknowledging the information available, and then choosing a response.

Part of being able to do this, of being able to stop yourself from reacting instinctively and therefore giving away your power, is to know yourself. Know the things you find hard to resist, know the things that irritate and anger you, know the times when you're at your most vulnerable to unguarded thoughts and reactions, and then make your best effort to manage yourself so that you are able to pause and give your best response to any circumstance, rather than your immediate worst reaction. Knowing when you're most likely to react to stimuli in a negative way, or which stimuli are most likely to cause a negative reaction, enables you to take extra care in those situations. For example, understanding that you can be grumpy when you're tired or hungry, enables you to take extra care when you are feeling less than rested or underfed.

To be best capable of responding with intent rather than responding on autopilot, requires us to have a toolkit of techniques that we can employ to help us interrupt the negative reflexive process of input and output. Key among these is slowing down – and that means everything from the way we go about our business, to the way we think about things and the way we interact with people.

Slowing down doesn't necessarily mean things should take longer, but it requires conscientious awareness of our routines, ourselves and our situation, so that we can build in breathing space to allow us to do everything on purpose, in a measured way, and avoid taking action on the spot, last minute, or in an uncontrolled manner. That goes for our internal processes (i.e. emotional responses) as well as our day-to-day tasks in work and in life.

Slowing down can involve pausing before you reply to a text message. It can involve reading through a brief the night before so that you are aware of what's required in the morning. Or it can involve building a pause into your mental processes so that when someone challenges you with a seemingly loaded question or enquiry, you don't immediately feel undermined, flustered, and forced to give a response that doesn't serve your best interests.

We've already mentioned the power of taking a breath, and when we build the intentional act of breathing into our input/output process, we take back control of our situation, are beholden to no-one, and get to choose our responses.

I haven't chosen the act of breathing at random. Breathing is a powerful tool, and experiments with breathing techniques have produced astounding results in many different fields, from sport to pain control, hypnosis to concentration. Breathing is the foundation for meditation, it is the foundation for how our bodies work, and it is the foundation for staying in control.

Beyond this, breathing is a way of connecting with the wider energy of the Universe. When we consciously and intentionally draw in air from the atmosphere around us, we are making a connection to the world, in just the same way we connect to the ground beneath our feet when we walk. When we stop to breathe, we are connected to the energy of the Universe, we are drawing atoms into bodies that were born in the hearts of stars, just as every atom in our body was. When we breathe, we are not simply catching our breath, but we are cleansing ourselves, interfacing with the infinite, finding our place within it – and as part of it.

When we stop to breathe – and make use of that pause – we can put this moment into the context of the infinite. Most negativity becomes petty and meaningless when considered in relation to the vastness of the Universe and existence itself. So when you're tempted to give your workmate an earful because they've taken the last doughnut, or flash your lights at the driver who cut in front of you, just breathe, connect to the Universe and put it in context. And by the time you've done that you'll have either thought of a much more graceful response instead of that knee-jerk negative reaction, or the moment will have passed. In any case, you'll feel much calmer and at peace.

When we feel worried, anxious or find ourselves put on the spot, we can use calm, controlled breathing to centre ourselves and return to the present. We can use breathing to allay fear and slow a panicked heartbeat. And we can use breathing after the input to pause and let us choose our own output. But most of all we can use breathing to allow us to connect with the energy of the divine Universe and recognise our place within it and as part of it.

Next time you feel yourself on the verge of giving away your power by reacting to a negative situation, stop, breathe, retain your power and choose a response instead. And then feel your energy grow stronger and stronger as you connect with the divine.

CHAPTER RECAP

When we react negatively to situations on autopilot, too often we give away our power and weaken ourselves. If we can interrupt the input/output process using a technique such as breathing, we can choose an appropriate response instead, and strengthen ourselves by growing our power.

It always better to respond with positive intent that to react with a negative reflex.

CHAPTER 13: WHO DO YOU SERVE?

"Responsibility to yourself means refusing to let others do your thinking, talking and naming for you; it means learning to respect and use your own brains and instincts." – Adrienne Rich

We spend our lives being told what to do. When we're toddlers we have to behave and do as our parents tell us otherwise we get into trouble. Then we go to kindergarten and we have to behave and do as our teachers tell us so that we don't get into trouble. Then we move into big school, and there's another teacher, who stands at the front of the class, and we have to behave and do as they say, so that we don't get into trouble. If we decide to go to college, we have a lecturer and another set of rules, and we have to behave and do what we're told so that we don't get into trouble. And then if we're lucky enough to get a job we have a boss who stands in front of us, and we have to behave and do as we're told so that we don't get into trouble.

Throughout our lives, we put these other people at the centre of our Universe, we become unable to function without these people giving us instructions, and we fear them because they have power over us. They have control over whether we have a pleasant day or a horrible day, and as we've touched upon, we are programmed to live in fear of unpleasant experiences. And so we show them gratitude when they praise us, and we are apologetic when the work we do or the way we behave doesn't please them. We are beholden that they are blessing us with the kindness of paying our wages, of allowing us to go a day without a confrontation, that they allow us to keep doing the work we are expected to do. We pray that if we keep our head down, if we colour between the lines and do what we're told, these people will bless us with a day without grief, the same old same old, the status quo.

We spend our lives being afraid of these people, deferring to their authority, and this spills over into our daily lives. We become beholden not just to our bosses or our teachers, but also to the shopkeeper, the person on the street, the driver of that other car, the policeman, the librarian, that person who is taller than us, older than us, more serious or competent than us. Anyone – everyone – has the potential to give us an unpleasant experience, so we avoid eye contact, tiptoe through the world, and put everyone else on a pedestal because, after all, they have power over us.

But at what point do we stop putting others at the centre of our Universe, constantly giving our power away to them, and instead put ourselves at the centre of our Universe? At what point do we stop being beholden to others, and become beholden just to ourselves?

This isn't a suggestion to ignore the rule of law, or to be badly behaved in school or at work, but when we put ourselves at the centre of our Universe we act in the best interests of ourselves and others not because we fear that person who is in authority and their ability to ruin our day, but because we have the integrity to know that it's the best course of action. We begin to approach our work with the intention of doing a good job, instead of avoiding a bad experience. We start to colour outside the lines because sometimes that's what it takes to make something great, instead of staying safely within the lines and being mediocre.

Indeed, there will be times when the course of action which we deem to be the best, the most appropriate, may not be the course that others would have chosen. It may even fall outside 'the rules' and get us into trouble, but because now we are beholden only to ourselves, because we have acted with integrity and without being beholden to others, we know that we have acted in the best and most proper way. No one builds statues of people who follow the rules.

When we put ourselves at the centre of our Universe, when we chose to be beholden only to ourselves and not to others, then we choose not to require the permission or approval of others but only of ourselves. With this, however, comes responsibility. We must understand that if we are not going to seek the approval or permission of others than we must have faith in our own integrity and our ability to make the right decisions. We must respect the right of others to disagree, but we must also acknowledge that we are only looking to ourselves for permission and have the confidence and integrity to guide ourselves in this respect. This can be scary at times because it requires that we step outside our comfort zones and step up to the challenge, but it is important that we have enough faith in ourselves to be able to make decisions and take action even when the thing we're doing goes against what others may consider to be correct, and certainly doesn't meet with their approval or permission.

You don't need to be Rosa Parks, refusing to give up your seat to a white passenger in the coloured section of the bus – a rebellious act of civil disobedience that became a symbol of the growing civil rights movement. You don't have need to be Emmeline Pankhurst, whose militant actions played a key role in gaining women the right to vote. You don't have to change the world (although the world will always need more people like Parks and Pankhurst), but you must have enough faith in your own ability to make the right decision that you are able to change your world.

I'll give you an example that is so far removed from world-changers like Rosa Parks and Emmeline Pankhurst that you'd think I was talking about a different subject altogether, but it highlights the point about having faith in your own ability to make decisions and act in the same way, but from the opposite end of the spectrum.

I spent some time living alone in a small town outside London, where I was working as an editor for a variety of trade and hobbyist magazines. I put everyone else on a pedestal, at the centre of my Universe, to the point where I was so undermined I had no faith in my own ability to make decisions or take action. I sought approval for everything, because over the years I'd allowed my self-confidence and self-esteem to be eroded until I had no faith in myself or the value of my decisions.

This lack of faith became so bad that it turned into a kind of obsessive compulsive disorder. If I had been ironing a shirt in the morning, I would have to stop my journey to work and return to my house several times to check that I had turned the iron off, because I didn't trust myself to have done it. And after doing that several times, and assuring myself that the iron was off and unplugged and that the house wasn't going to burn to the ground, I then had to return several times to make sure I'd shut all the windows. And after that I had to return to ensure that the front door was locked.

I had no faith in myself. Even though I knew I had unplugged the iron, closed the windows, locked the door – I still didn't trust myself that I had done those things. I didn't believe it. Without someone telling me that they were done and with a voice in my head telling me I couldn't be trusted with the responsibility to do those things, I had to return multiple times until I was convinced beyond reasonable doubt that the iron was off, the windows were shut, and the front door was locked.

And can you guess how many times I had forgotten to unplug the iron? Not once. Can you guess how often I'd left the windows open? Never. And can you guess how often I had left the front door unlocked? I never had.

It wasn't until I put myself at the centre of my Universe, that I started to have faith in my ability to make decisions for myself, without the approval of others. But it didn't happen overnight. It started one day, when I decided to bet on myself, and I discovered that my house didn't burn down. The next day I took a chance on myself and found that my door wasn't wide open when I returned from work. And slowly but surely, I started to learn that I didn't need anyone else's approval or permission, and that I was capable to making my own decisions and had enough faith in myself to trust that they were the right decisions. With each little leap of faith I realised that I was competent, I was capable and I wasn't going to burn my world down.

Of course, sometimes you don't make the right decisions. But this is the price of self-confidence and free will. Sometimes you will make the wrong decision, and you will have to deal with the outcome ('do the thing, have the power'), but consider this: Babe Ruth held the world record for the greatest number of home runs in baseball history and became known as the 'Home Run King'. But he was also known as the 'Strikeout King' having struck out an epic 1,330 times in his career. If he had let the fear of striking out stop him from going up to bat, he would never have won all those home runs which secured him a place in history.

We will look at the idea of approval and permission in decision making in the third section of the book, but for the moment let's work on putting ourselves at the centre of our Universe, and not giving away our power by allowing our Universe to revolve around others.

Before we do, though, we need to address selfishness. You may argue that putting ourselves at the centre of our Universe means being selfish, thinking of ourselves first, and disregarding the needs, wellbeing and emotions of others last, if at all. But it couldn't be further from the truth. Indeed, if we were to disregard others completely we wouldn't get anywhere in the life (after all we need to work with others every day), and it would also mean that our existence was unkind and uncaring which goes against the whole idea and message of this book (we'll talk more about kindness in the next chapter).

But right now, we're putting ourselves at the centre of our Universe, and we're doing that because, in truth, we can be totally sure of nothing but our own minds. We have put so much importance in the authority and superiority of other people, people we have put on a pedestal, when we have no real reason to believe that they are correct at all. We can't truly be sure of anything beyond the centre of our own Universe, because everything else is simply an electrical impulse. What we see is an impulse that travels from our seeing organs down the optic nerve to our brains. What we feel travels from our touching organs to our brains. What we taste is an impulse that travels from our tasting organ to our brains. What we hear travels from those ear-shaped organs on the sides of our head to our brains.

Can we really be sure of the validity of these things? In the very first chapter we discussed how a lifetime of experiences act like filters, lenses distorting how we view the world. And what about tinnitus? Ever had a ringing in the ears after going to a loud concert? You know that ringing noise isn't occurring out there in the real world, but you can hear it, nonetheless. How can we be sure that those other people are more correct in their actions or decisions than we are? Indeed, we must learn to have faith in our own decisions and actions above all others, as we have no real way of knowing anything else is correct at all – other than by judging it to be correct ourselves.

What we're talking about is basic solipsism, a branch of philosophy that explores the idea that nothing is certain apart from our own minds and that the external world, and indeed the minds of other people, cannot truly be known and may not even exist.

Yet we put so much importance on the views, authority and intelligence of others, at the expense of ourselves – we give up so much of our power to others – and the whole time all we can really be sure of is ourselves. We see other people as being confident, we see them as having their lives sorted, everything in balance, the perfect existence. But we don't see the turmoil behind the scenes, the financial insecurity, the emotional insecurity and the self-doubt. We create a picture of others that we have no way of knowing is real or not.

But what we do know without doubt is that our own existence is real. It stands to reason that we should have faith in ourselves and our abilities, act with the integrity to be the best version of ourselves, and have faith that the decisions we make and actions we take are the best for all involved. That we do a good job at work not because we have to, but because we want to, we are able to, it's the right thing to do, and we hold ourselves to high standards. And we are prepared to step up and do the best we can regardless of whether we will fail or not.

When we put ourselves at the centre of our Universe we are required to have faith in our own abilities, to understand where our abilities end, and to take responsibility for the state of our Universe and the way we exist within it. And that means honouring our best selves and showing ourselves the respect to do the best we can, always, everywhere.

CHAPTER RECAP

We cannot be sure of anything other than ourselves, yet we so often put much more importance on the ability of others to make decisions that we absolve ourselves of responsibility over our own lives, and let others have power over us. We put others on pedestals and subjugate ourselves. But when we have faith in ourselves and our ability to take action and make decisions, we put ourselves at the centre of our Universe and act not out of fear of reprimand, but because we know that we are doing the right thing.

CHAPTER 14: PUT KINDNESS FIRST

"Be kind whenever possible. It is always possible."
– His Holiness the Dalai Lama

I'd burned out running the publishing arm of a media company. So I quit and took a job working in a warehouse smashing up computers. I needed a job that wasn't cerebral and this was the perfect role. Old computers that needed to have their hard drives wiped so the data couldn't fall into the hands of fraudsters would come into the warehouse, where they were smashed up and recycled. I was a member of the team of smashers (not my official job title), a really satisfying job that required no skill, just protective clothing and goggles. And a large hammer.

Everyone who worked there had a story, just as everybody, everywhere does. You might think that the kind of person who does a job like that would be a bit of a failure at life. You might think they'd be unintelligent, uneducated. But if you were to think that, to judge someone on the job they do, you might need a lesson in kindness.

One day I got talking to one of my fellow smashers, a man who was older than me and who had just started in the role. I asked him what he did before he arrived there to wield a large hammer against outdated hardware.

He replied that he'd been working in Central America, where he'd spent ten years in charge of the day-to-day operations of twelve large international airports. When the contract came to an end and hadn't been renewed, he had to return to the UK, and the only job he could get was next to me, with a pair of protective goggles and a mallet.

Everyone has a story. It's part of what makes them who they are. Our stories include the experiences that make the filters through which we view ourselves and the world around us. We need to respect everyone's story just as we should respect our own. But when we act in a judgemental, unthinking way to other people, we do a disservice to their story. And when people are rude, or unkind, or mean to us, they do a disservice to our story, just as we do when we don't show kindness to ourselves.

I always pay attention to the safety announcement on an airplane. Most people don't. Most people have seen it before. Hundreds of times before. I've seen it hundreds of times before, but that's not why I pay attention to the member of cabin crew pointing out the exits and showing us how to put on a life jacket. I pay attention to the member of the cabin crew giving the presentation because they get paid very little and do a difficult job. I pay attention because they've been through tough training to save the lives of people like me. They've been dunked in pools of icy water to practice escaping from a plane that crashes into the sea. They endured friction burns practicing how to escape down the emergency slide from a burning aircraft. I pay attention out of respect for their story, and because I might learn something. Not about how to escape from the plane – I've seen that hundreds of times before. But I might learn something about another human being.

I pay attention because everyone has something to teach me. Everyone has a lifetime of experiences, layer upon layer of stories. I pay attention because people are interesting, and it's more interesting to learn something new from someone I haven't met, than it is to repeat my story, which I've already heard.

And I pay attention because I would want people to pay attention to me, to take a real interest in my story. One day I might have something important to say.

Our stories make us unique, complex creatures, like a beautiful rose with its petals curling round in delicate complex layers. I am like this, you are like this, everyone is like this. It makes us divine. And when you hear people greeting each other with the ancient Sanskrit word "namaste" they are literally saying "the divine within me bows down before the divine within you". When we encounter another person, we should remember to acknowledge their story, their complex layers, and show them the same reverence that we would wish someone would show us. The same respect. The same kindness.

"Namaste."

But perhaps you disagree. Perhaps you see kindness as a sign of weakness, and with all this talk of power something as weak as kindness shouldn't factor into the book anywhere. You might argue that power should be about being strong, you might argue, about putting your needs before those of others and that, in order to find your power, retain your power, and grow your power you need to be tough, like a warrior ready to do battle.

But you'd be wrong.

Kindness, compassion, empathy and love are the most powerful forces in the Universe. And when we act without them, we give away our power. When we are mean, we give away our power. When we are rude, unthinking, uncaring, we give away our power. When we are judgemental, sneering and ridiculing, we give away our power.

When we are selfish we give away our power.

Compassion and kindness not only allow us to grow by putting ourselves into the shoes of others and feel what they are feeling, but they also enable us to be flexible, to respond with compassion rather than to react with anger. When someone behaves badly toward us, we can imagine a reason beneath the action. And in doing so we become strong like a blade of grass that flexes gracefully in the fiercest wind, as opposed to the mighty oak tree which, unable to bend, breaks in half.

Compassion and kindness and empathy are constructive, creative forces, which enable us to do good. Whether that good act is one that changes the world, or simply a smile and a polite word to someone who needs it, kindness can go a long way. And it ripples outwards.

When I worked as a delivery driver, there would be times where, with a smile and a wave, I would stop to let another driver out of a side road, someone who had clearly been waiting a long time. And as I drove behind them, I would often see that they would stop to let another driver out at the next junction. And that driver would stop to let someone out at the junction after that, and so on and so on, a wave of goodwill and kindness travelling forwards and outwards and upwards, as each person paid it forward and their positive energy grew. And every time that someone would let me pull out at a busy junction in my van, I would wonder how long this chain of goodwill had been going and how much further it would continue.

On other days when the traffic was at its most congested, and everybody was angry because they were late getting home for their dinner, they wouldn't let anybody out at the junction, and instead we'd all be waiting for what seemed like an eternity.

Traffic is a perfect metaphor for the role that kindness plays in the art of graceful living. Traffic works at its best when we all show kindness and consideration to others. Like one of those Georgian ballroom dances that we see in the movies where people elegantly waltz around each other in the wonderfully ornate ballroom, traffic – like life – flows well when it is a dance of kindness, and when we respectfully consider everyone else we all get home on time.

But when you get those drivers who just want to mosh, who just want to jump around and dance by and for themselves, who are unable or unwilling to conceive the dances that anyone else is dancing and bump into anyone who dares to get in their way – then we all get home late for our dinner.

This mangle of metaphors is about the role that kindness plays in growing our power as individuals and as collective humans. The world won't end because of compassion and kindness. Kindness and compassion don't cause poverty, disease, famine. These are constructive forces that bond us together, that say your pain is my pain and together we are stronger. They are creative forces that say your dream is my dream, together we can put a man on the moon, or explore the deepest oceans, or build something magnificent and wonderful.

Kindness, compassion, empathy are the three words that are mightier than any sword, and if nurtured and allowed to flourish, will grow your power more than anything else. Your power, my power. Everyone's power.

Being kind means giving people the benefit of the doubt, laughing with people rather than at them, refusing to ridicule others, and refusing to judge other people until you know their story. Judging other people is one of the most negative acts that any of us can do, but unfortunately it has become a national pastime that drains our power as we discovered in chapter six when we learned to stop complaining. And when we stop judging people, not only do we start to appreciate the good in everyone, but we grow the good within ourselves.

This is perfectly highlighted by the phrase coined by American author and columnist Dave Barry, who said "if someone is nice to you but rude to the waiter, they are not a nice person."

Think about it. Einstein started his career as a patent clerk. Whoopi Goldberg worked as mortician. Warren Beatty worked as a rat catcher. Brad Pitt even spent a stint dressed up in a chicken suit handing out fliers for a fried chicken joint. The man smashing up computers next to me in that warehouse was responsible for the operation of twelve airports.

When we share our strength, and take our time and energy to help others, to be considerate and kind – even when we do so anonymously and with no obvious gain to ourselves – our power grows, and it does so in the form of integrity and spiritual energy. Just as a candle can be used to light a thousand more candles and its own light never diminishes, yet the light grows stronger. If we are tender and thoughtful in our treatment of others, if we tread lightly upon the earth, and if we show kindness to all around, including ourselves, then our power grows within and it ripples outwards.

When we put kindness at the centre of our life we choose to see through the eyes of others before we react against them, then we can choose to respond with sympathy, or at the very least with understanding. That doesn't mean we should be either weak or meek, but it does require us to be brothers or sisters in the family of mankind, and careful caretakers of the planet we are currently inhabiting.

We have that choice, and we have that power.

Be powerful. Be kind.

CHAPTER RECAP

Kindness is one of the most powerful forces there is. Kindness enables us to see through the eyes of others before we judge them or their actions, and enables us to feel what others feel as if we were them. When we act with kindness – even when there is no obvious personal gain for ourselves – our power not only increases in terms of inner integrity, but it ripples outwards, becoming stronger as it spreads.

CHAPTER 15: KEEP YOUR BALANCE

"Only when moving can one comfortably maintain one's balance."
– Albert Einstein

I was an editor of a glossy magazine, and I was working late at night on my second book in my office in Manhattan, with a view of the Chrysler building. An Englishman in New York, it sounds pretty cool doesn't it? I was flying high. I was one of those people who just seemed to move from success to success.

Except I wasn't. I'd allowed my life to get out of balance.

The book would never get written. I was deeply unhappy. And I was so broke I didn't have a penny to my name. I couldn't afford food and I was starving. I was so hungry that I was living on the microwave popcorn that came free when we ordered stationary for the office. The office kitchen had two microwaves and I had them both running, with my popcorn dinner expanding in front of my eyes. I switched on the electric kettle to make a cup of coffee and suddenly found myself plunged into pitch black darkness. I'd fused the entire building.

All around me were the sounds of New York City, the noise of the traffic, of the cabs beeping their horns, sounds of the hustle and bustle of four million people going somewhere, yet I felt like I was going nowhere. In a city of a million flashing lights I was lost in a black hole of darkness. I had evaporated into nothing the moment that fuse blew.

I was a mess and I could feel my power seeping away night after night, as I stared at my blank computer screen, without a clue what to write. I had been so focused on one area of my existence that I had failed to take responsibility for another. My career seemed to be going ok, but financially I was falling apart. This was a juggling act and I had dropped a ball.

When we lose sight of our personal bigger picture, as I had done by spreading myself too thin, we give away our power. When we hide from reality, seeking sanctuary in the things that are easy to control or that bring us instant gratification, pretending that the things we've given up all responsibility for don't matter or don't exist, we are out of control. When we focus so much on our career, but we don't have any clean clothes to wear, or we only see our loved ones for thirty minutes a day. When we take comfort in food, or alcohol or drugs and become unhealthy, and our work and relationships suffer. We become addicted to exercise, to slimming, to sport or anything which comes at the expense of another area of our lives, we lose our power and things start to fall apart.

For a life that's healthy in all its areas, a life that's lived on purpose, we need to maintain our balance and keep all our balls in the air. We need to identify the different roles that we have, the different identities we have within those roles, and the different responsibilities we have under those identities. You might be a manager at work, but you might also be a wife at home, you might be running a business in your spare time, but you might also be a parent – and you are also the centre of your own personal Universe. You have responsibilities to your job, to your home life, to your side projects and to yourself. And when you can identify all your roles and responsibilities, you find yourself in a position where you are more able to maintain balance. And when you can maintain balance you can grow your power in all those areas.

Here's an exercise that helps to maintain this balance. Sit down with your notebook – you know, the one you've been writing your daily gratitude in – and list your roles and identities. They may be just like the three I outlined above (work, home, personal). There may be others. Perhaps you play on a sports team. Perhaps you're a parent. Perhaps you are a member of a charitable organisation in your spare time. Perhaps your financial responsibilities need to factor in there, or your responsibilities to the people you care for, or who care for you.

Get your notebook, and note these identities down, and the responsibilities you have under all of them. As we've done with all the exercises in this notebook, keep it positive – it's not a job description, it's a motivational document – and then cement it in your mind. This should be about empowerment, so it's important that you don't see all these roles as things that are overwhelming and frightening, but see the exercise as something to empower you and make you stronger, better and more capable. This is your personal mission statement and it might look something like this:

- PROFESSIONAL

  To be financially secure, having achieved this
  stability doing things I enjoy and which I'm good at,
  through multiple streams of income.

- HUSBAND

  To nurture my relationship with my partner and
  enable it to grow stronger every day. To love and to
  support, to carry my share of the burden, and to
  create a home sanctuary away from the stresses of
  the working day.

- PERSONAL

  To be confident, emotionally stable, in charge of
  myself, constantly working to better myself, to have
  faith in my own decisions and to grow constantly in
  every direction.

When you've built your mission statements for the
different roles that you inhabit, stop and take a look.
Understand where your responsibilities lie, and honestly
think about whether you are, in this moment, aware of
where you stand in each of them.

There will be times when one role will require more
attention than others for prolonged periods of time.
Maybe a project at work requires longer hours than
normal, maybe a personal goal needs attention, but if
you are mindful of your other roles, then you can
temporarily move your focus into the areas that require

them, without dropping the ball in the other areas. You may have to let people who are important to you know that your attention may be focused elsewhere for a period of time. You may need to put in place measures so that the other areas of your life don't suffer when you need to direct your attention elsewhere. Perhaps you will need to arrange for someone to take your place at charity meetings. Perhaps you will need to book time away from work.

There will be times when you will feel overwhelmed as if you are losing your balance. But stay mindful, don't be afraid, and take stock of what's going on. If you need to bring your attention back to an area that is suffering, then do so. As the saying goes, "everything will be alright in the end – if it's not alright, it's not the end." There is always time to address the balance, and if you're mindful of your responsibilities in each role, you'll know when your attention is needed in any given area. And as your ability to juggle increases, you will feel ever more empowered to build your roles, add layers, and become even more of a do-er than you already are.

But, and there's always a 'but', as with every aspect of this book, you mustn't become complacent, as there are forces that will sabotage you. Many of these forces come from within, and will strike you when you are tired, unwell, badly nourished or suffering from the effects of alcohol or drugs. We'll talk more about this in section three, but needless to say, you will be more able to keep all your balls in the air if you are fit, healthy, and nourished in mind, body and spirit. Looking after yourself and focusing on your own wellbeing will ensure your capacity and capability in all other areas of your life.

In section three we'll also look at how you can organise yourself, how you can plan ahead, and how you can master the mundane aspects of life in order to meet the responsibilities of your roles and then go beyond them. But to do this and to remain balanced, we must be fearless in doing 'the thing'.

When we do it, we will have the power.

CHAPTER RECAP

We have different identities, and different roles and responsibilities for each of them. But when we allow them to fall out of balance, the entirety of our life suffers. By mindfully being aware of all aspects of our life, and where our responsibilities lie, we can choose to move focus from one to another when needed, without neglecting any of them. When we are mindfully aware of our whole picture, we can act to master all roles, without sacrificing any.

CHAPTER 16: DON'T GET TRAPPED BY THE PROCESS

"I am not a robot. I have a heart and I bleed."
– Serena Williams

I was working for a multimillion pound national organisation. It was a logistics company that had distribution centres across the UK, and it was a model of efficiency. The whole business was built around processes that made operations lean, effective and kept the profits rolling in. These processes were fundamental to the organisation's growth and success, and everyone in the business, from the shop floor right up to senior management had their daily tasks and routines mapped out in detail in a series of process trees that described their function and their duties. It was smart, it was efficient, it was ahead of its time.

But it was also a ball and chain.

Whenever I suggested improvements that could be made to an area of the business, they went nowhere. The people involved were unable to consider them because that kind of decision making didn't fit anywhere in their process trees. They were powerless to embrace opportunities or change. The very systems that had been designed to make the organisation groundbreaking and market-leading were also holding it back. Processes that are too rigid can be detrimental to the wellbeing of the organisation.

In chapter one I told you that to reach your goals you had to let them go and put your faith in the process. But if a process becomes too rigid, if we learn to rely it on too much, then it becomes a crutch and it can steal our power as we are unable to adapt ourselves to any changing environment or circumstances that we find ourselves in. We might be faced with unexpected life events or changes in our situation that we could not have foreseen or planned for. And our processes may not be flexible enough to cope.

At times like this we must embrace our humanity and turn to our integrity. We are not robots on a production line, following a regimented string of computer code. We are people. We are flexible, malleable, and as we have discovered we also have the strength to understand that life will throw us curveballs that require us to step outside the comfort of our process, to adapt to what incident or change of fortune may come our way. And we must partner that flexibility with the strength to either return to the process of reaching our goals at a later time, or adapt our process and our goals to accommodate this new information or circumstance.

When we live life on purpose, when we have the integrity to act only in beneficial ways, embracing kindness, strength, and an understanding of our bigger picture, we can flex like a blade of grass, we can adjust, adapt, and grow stronger than ever by not allowing our very own process to become a prison from which we cannot escape.

Life is not a straight road, but an uncharted journey that

requires constant course correction and adjustment. Even the most well-planned route cannot account for all the obstacles we come across on the way. We must be able to go over, go around, go under or go through when we are required to do so, sometimes at a moment's notice. And with the flexibility to step away from our process and the strength and integrity to return to it later, and the faith in ourselves to know that all won't be lost when we step off the path, we can do just that. But if we are unable to flex, to adjust and reroute, our process will keep us bumping against that first obstacle forever.

CHAPTER RECAP

While falling in love with the process helps us to move towards our goals, and be better versions of ourselves and our lives, we must not become dependent on it, otherwise we are no longer its master and the process instead starts to own us. We must be flexible enough to be able to step away from our process when called to do so, but strong enough to return or change our process when the time is right. Our process must serve us, not the other way around.

PART 3: GROW YOUR POWER

CHAPTER 17: GROW YOUR POWER

"You can't pour from an empty jug." – proverb

By now you should understand that we're on a journey – engaged in a process that is about ongoing improvement, about shedding the skin of our old disempowered selves and revealing the strengths, attributes and potential that we've always had, but which we've failed to recognise and enjoy because they've been hidden. But now that we're casting aside those insecurities that we have created within ourselves, the layers of untruths that we've piled on top of ourselves, and we are rejecting the negative influences of ourselves and those around us who seek to undermine us or use our capacity for their own agendas, we are suddenly able to see what we have to offer, and what an uninhibited life lived at a higher level can look like.

We have learned that we have power, so long as we can interrupt the programming that has stifled it. We have learned that we can stop our power being hijacked by the negativity of ourselves and others, by the self-talk, the negative agendas, and the attachments we create to those forces that prevent us from developing self-reliance, self-esteem, self-confidence, and faith in ourselves. And we've learned that we've had this power all along. It's always been with us, but we needed to be proactive in releasing it and engaging with it.

Now the time has come to build upon this foundation, to nurture and grow this power. It's time to use it to create the life we want, to be the kind of person we want to be, and to partake in the fine art of graceful living.

As we discussed in the last section, this may seem like a selfish exercise, but it isn't. By growing to be the best we can be, by continuing our journey, we will not only nurture a better version of ourselves that is capable, confident and that benefits from the joy of life, but we will become strong within ourselves, and kind, empathic and nurturing to those around us. We will help others to grow while we learn from them and in turn share with them what we've learned. We will understand the problems faced by others as we have been through their journey ourselves, and we will understand that sometimes there is more to be gained from genuinely listening than from simply waiting for our turn to speak.

In this final section of the book, we move beyond just developing the ability to 'deal with it' to increasing our power by taking care of ourselves physically, mentally and spiritually. We will look at ways to become more effective at taking action, at mastering the things that require our attention every day, and then making space to do the extraordinary and work towards our goals. It stands to reason that when we are not operating at our best, we cannot help ourselves and we cannot help others. By interrupting the unnecessary negative thoughts that lead to unnecessary emotional reactions, we can instead objectively look at ourselves, our situations, and see our place in the world. That's not to say we should stifle our emotions, but when they come from a less subjective place, they become more authentic, valuable and effective.

By being at our best physically, we can better serve ourselves mentally, and when we are at our best mentally, we can better serve ourselves emotionally and spiritually. And then we can better serve our goals, and those around us. By living our lives gracefully and on purpose, we can develop positive practices that ensure we are confident and capable in the decisions we make, the steps forward that we take, and the very existence that we lead.

So now that we are less constrained by the restrictive forces of insecurity, anxiety and undermining influences, let's examine how we can nurture even greater strength through wellbeing, measured action and self-care. Let's grow our power.

CHAPTER 18: WHAT'S YOUR EXCUSE?

"Ninety-nine percent of the failures come from people who have the habit of making excuses." – George Washington Carver

Life sucks. Other people have all the luck. It's not fair. He's better looking than me. She's got nicer hair than me. It's ok for them, they've got rich parents. They're just talented like that. He's cleverer than me, taller than me, doesn't have the problems that I have. He gets it. Why do bad things always happen to me? If that hadn't happened all those years ago, I wouldn't be in this terrible position. It's not my fault. It's their fault. It's her fault. It's his fault. It is my fault. It's all my fault. I'm just not very good. I'm not tall enough. I'm too short. I'm too fat. I'm too stupid. I'm too lazy. I'm too negative. I'm too white. I'm too black. I'm too blonde. I'm too tall. I'm too arrogant. I'm too ugly. I was born this way. I'll never achieve anything. I'm a failure. I'm unpopular. I'm not very likeable. I'm universally hated. I'm in a world that hates me. I'm in a Universe that won't let me succeed. I'm doomed to failure for the rest of my life. I wish I was dead. I hate myself. I deserve to fail. I deserve all the bad things that happen to me. I just don't get it.

Life sucks.

Sound familiar? Remember all those negative thoughts that we spent so much time trying to banish in the first section of this book? Those thoughts which our new approach to life will help us to keep at bay if we maintain the proper attitude and approach to living from this day forward? If we are pro-active and work to keep our power and not give it away?

How many of those negative thoughts do you think are excuses? How many of those thoughts give you a reason for not trying that thing, for not taking responsibility for your situation, for your outcomes? How often do you find yourself making excuses for things not turning out the way you want, or for not even trying in the first place?

There's a comfort to be found in our rut, in the place where we're stuck. Like a comfort blanket our perceived obstacles keep us safe from failure. We can't fail if we never try, our excuses reassure us, but in truth by not trying we've already failed.

"I'm not wealthy enough", our excuses tell us. "I'm not as clever as they are"; "I'm not tall enough"; "Last time I tried that it all went wrong"; "I don't have the safety net they have"; "I don't have the energy"; "I don't have the patience."

We use our negative perspective as evidence for not taking action, when all we're doing is using it as an excuse to be lazy. An excuse to do nothing. Doing nothing and doing something both take the same amount of time – but one of them will take you forward, and the other will take you backwards. One of them requires action and builds muscle, while the other promotes inaction and makes your muscles atrophy.

What other excuses do you use? Do you ever find yourself saying you don't have time? That you'll do that thing as soon as you've finished this other thing (a thing that you're unlikely to ever finish)? That it seems too much like hard work? That you'll just have a quick sit down and a cup of coffee before you get started on that thing you've been putting off for months?

If you start to think about it, we make excuses in every aspect of our lives. Sometimes we use genuine excuses to avoid doing things we don't want to do, that aren't beneficial to us, and we call these excuses 'reasons'. But sometimes we confuse genuine 'reasons' with excuses. The reasons we often give for not doing those things, those things that may or may not lead us to greatness and the life we've always dreamed of, are actually just excuses. Excuses because we're comfortable in our unhappy rut. Excuses because we're frightened of trying and failing (when really, we fail whenever we don't try). Excuses because it requires effort, and requires us to take responsibility for the outcome. Excuses because we're lazy.

And we're lazy because we've made too many excuses in the past and now the muscles we use for doing things – for taking action – have atrophied. Excuses give us a reason to stay safe within our ever-shrinking comfort zone. Excuses give us a reason to keep seeing the same results day after day, year after year.

Excuses give us a reason to do nothing.

Find a piece of paper and a pen – we're going to do another mental exercise. This time we're not writing in our notebook, because our notebook is for positive things only – it's a glowing beacon of positivity. In this exercise, we're working to banish excuses, so we're doing it on a separate piece of paper instead. And at the end we're going to rip it up, scrunch up all the pieces and throw them in the bin. Or you can burn them if you like, but remember – safety first.

Before you start writing on this bit of paper you're going to think about all the things that you would like to get done, all the projects you'd like to undertake, all the skills you'd like to learn, all the things that will help you to grow, develop, achieve. The book you'd like to write. The business you'd like to start. The DIY project you'd like to finally begin – or finish. Think about all those things you've been wanting to do, those things that will make you feel so pleased with yourself, so accomplished, if only you could start.

And then, on that piece of paper, write down all your excuses. Think of all the 'reasons' that you've used to stop yourself from doing them. Perhaps you think you don't have time to build that treehouse for your children. Perhaps you worry what your friends will think if you take dance classes. Perhaps you don't have the money. Write it down.

Keep writing. Think of all the reasons you've ever given yourself for not doing something new, those projects, those ideas, for not pushing the boundaries of your comfort zone. Get it all down on that piece of paper. Completely absorb yourself in the process, writing on both sides of the page, fill in all the gaps, if you need to get another piece of paper, do it, and keep writing until there are no excuses left, until all you've got in front of you are pages covered from top to bottom with ink.

This is where the exercise gets symbolic. Starting at the top corner of your page of excuses, tear off a tiny little piece. Then tear off another little piece. Take your time, give it your full focus, and bit-by-bit start ripping up those excuses. If you find your mind wandering, bring it back to the act in hand, and keep ripping until all you're left with is a pile of a thousand little bits of paper.

And then, one by one, take each little bit and roll it into a tiny excuse-ball. Give it your full attention just as you did before, and slowly, mindfully, build yourself a pile of tiny little excuse balls. And when you're done, pick them all up and throw them in the bin.

Or burn them.

Just don't burn your house down in the process.

What you've just done is mentally clear out all your excuses. And the next time you think of doing something, but find an excuse popping into your head, posing as a 'reason', you'll be able to recognise what it is and mentally throw it in the bin. When you no longer have excuses you are left with no choice but to take action. And when you take action, that's when things start to happen. That's when real change occurs.

And where we once had excuses that stopped us from starting, we must now employ resourcefulness to get things done. We must make the effort to find ways of getting started and proving those excuses wrong.

This book took over two years to write, but more than half of that time was spent finding excuses not to start. In the end, I had to become resourceful enough to keep those excuses at bay. One of my excuses was that I didn't have a laptop. I banished that excuse and wrote this book on my smartphone. When I worked in the call centre I would jot down ideas in 24-second chunks while I waited for someone to pick up the phone on the other end of the line. I would write in my lunch breaks. I would write on my phone while my delivery van was parked by the side of the road and I took my twenty-minute break.

When you no longer have excuses you are left with no choice but to take action.
Actions can be huge, or they can be tiny, but even if you're doing something small and seemingly insignificant – like hanging up your clothes instead of dumping them in a pile in the corner of your bedroom – you're flexing your muscles, getting stronger and growing your power. You are getting better; your life is getting better. Slowly but surely, you're coming unstuck, moving forward, becoming the best version of yourself.

Now that you don't have any excuses, you're ready to look at how you can use constructive action to always be improving, to be consciously building benefits and growth into your way of life. And life is no longer something that just happens to you, instead you are moving into a place where you are embracing the art of graceful living. You are like a trophy-winning jockey moving up the field, riding your horse to victory. You are winning.

It's time to learn how to use your power to bend life to your will, to grow your power so that you become a better version of yourself, and to shape your life to look more like the life you've dreamed about.

Forward.

CHAPTER RECAP

Excuses give us a reason to do nothing. We hide behind them because it's easier than doing something. But when you get rid of your excuses you have no choice but to act. When you get rid of your excuses you become resourceful and things will start to happen.

So, what are you waiting for? Get rid of your excuses.

CHAPTER 19: SUPERCHARGE YOUR STATE

"To be prepared is half the victory." – Miguel De Cervantes

I was a professional photographer and I had been assigned to photograph a television presenter. He was well known in the UK for his shows about property, and when I met him I was amazed at how big he was. Not only was he a lot taller than he appeared on TV, but his arms were like tree trunks. He clearly spent time in the gym.

The photoshoot was outdoors and quite informal. It was just the two of us and we got chatting as we strolled from location to location to location, stopping to shoot some pictures whenever we came to an interesting spot. Getting a good conversation going really helps a photoshoot because it builds rapport, puts you both at ease, and I'm always intrigued to learn the story of the person I'm photographing.

Everyone's got a story. Whether it's the celebrity movie star or the postman who brings your letters, all our lives are adventures – and if you listen well and ask the right questions, you'll learn that everyone has a fascinating tale to tell. You do. I do. Everyone does.

Eventually I steered the conversation to exercise – I'm fascinated by the personal regimes of people who seem so fit, healthy and successful. He explained that wherever they were filming the show, whichever part of the country, he insisted that the hotel he was staying in had a gym. If he couldn't do even a short workout in the morning he could almost guarantee that he would start the day feeling grumpy, that the day's filming would be slow and hard work, and that he'd be ineffective not just as a television presenter, but in terms of dealing with all the mundanities of everyday life.

On the other hand, if he could fit in a workout before breakfast, he could fly through the day in a good mood, get everything done easily and without any drama, and be efficient and proactive in getting everything else done that needed doing. This one small activity, carried out as part of his daily routine enabled him to operate at his best, to be proactive, productive, and to have the inner power to be the master of his day and of himself.

Growing our power means finding ways to be the master of ourselves, and not being at the mercy of our negative thoughts, our emotions, or allowing people or situations to 'push our buttons'. And it means developing techniques that we can employ to not just retain our power, but to put ourselves in states where we are most effective, or most powerful.

As I've mentioned throughout this book, when we talk about our power, we are using it as shorthand for our strength, our mastery of ourselves and the situations we find ourselves in, and our ability to take action that is beneficial to ourselves, those around us and the wider world.

To be able to operate in the most effective way at any given time, to be able to respond with measure, elegance and grace instead of reacting reflexively, to take positive action instead of procrastinating, to move forward and partake in the fine art of living and to 'do the thing', we must be in a state where we can harness our power. And to be in such a state, where we are most powerful, we must find techniques that put us there.

We've all experienced days where we're not in the best state and not feeling powerful. Ever arrived at work tired, moody, or just not feeling it? Ever had 'meh' days? Ever had days where a hangover has made you feel anxious, paranoid or just less capable of working at your best? Ever drunk too much coffee and found yourself twitchy and insecure? Ever been so exhausted you've not known what was going on around you?

If you can say yes to any of the above then you know the benefit of being in a good state mentally, physically and emotionally. But how do you go about taking ownership of your state, taking action to improve your state, or indeed using techniques – just like the television presenter in my photoshoot – to immediately change your state so that you're always operating at your best?

Chances are you probably already use different techniques to change your state. Who doesn't have a cup of tea or coffee first thing in the morning to help them wake up and become alert? Many people enjoy a glass of wine or beer at the end of the week to help them unwind. Both methods have their pros and cons –

you wouldn't want to knock back a couple of beers before giving a presentation to the board of directors, and you wouldn't want to drink a double espresso last thing at night. But there are other tools you can employ when you need to give yourself a kick start and energise your thinking, your presence in the moment – and change your state.

Fundamental to these are a strong foundation of wellness – be well rested, be hydrated, be nourished, don't be hung over and try to have a balanced blood sugar level. But there are always going to be times where these things are out of balance or, let's be honest, you're just not feeling it.

So, when you wake up and you find yourself thinking "what's the point?" how do you go about changing your state in an instant, so that you're firing on all cylinders?

Tony Robbins, Tim Ferriss and Mel Robbins are all proponents of using physical actions to trigger an emotional and mental change, and this is one of the best ways to change your mood, engage your brain, snap out of any funk you might be in and snap in to an effective state. Every morning Tony Robbins dunks himself in a pool of icy water for 30 seconds to wake himself up and get the blood pumping. If you've ever been on holiday somewhere with a swimming pool or near the sea, you'll know that a quick splash is a great way to help you wake you up and start the day. Ferriss, too, suggests a short cold shower to start the morning, while Mel Robbins recommends counting from 5 down to 1 and then simply moving to create the impetus for action. I've met people who start their day with a workout or a 10k run to get them in the right frame of mind for an effective and productive day ahead.

But what works for you? Not everyone has access to a plunge pool or a cold shower at a moment's notice, and not everyone is able to jump up and down on a mini trampoline outside the office, as Tony Robbins does before he goes on stage. But clearly some sort of physical action, something that can jolt the brain from a low state and get it operating at a higher level in a matter of moments, can be a simple but effective state-changing technique.

Some people practice the art of ecstatic dance. Less an art, more just a moment of release, it's about going to a place where you can either be alone (ie. your living room), or where you don't feel judged, putting on some music that moves you, and dancing as if nobody's watching. Just let go, and let your limbs move freely to the music. Let go of your ego, forget about what people think, and dance like a whirling dervish.

But if you're at work and you can't leap about to loud music, is there somewhere private you can go and do ten star jumps before you have to give that presentation? Can you find somewhere to do ten quick press-ups and get the blood pumping? Or perhaps something more subtle that you can do at your desk – a simple breathing exercise, and adjusting your posture in the same way that Bowa taught me to introduce a gap between stimulus and response in Indonesia.

As I learned when I photographed that television

presenter, a physical workout in the morning is a great way to put yourself in a positive state for the day, and the added benefits of exercise are so widely known I don't need to go into them here. But sometimes we may not have able to do a workout, or sometimes the change you are looking for might be more intellectual than physical.

One obvious way to change your state is to make yourself feel good by looking good. Putting on a nice outfit or spending a therapeutic evening grooming yourself with a hot bath and a face-pack is a way to put yourself into a relaxed, de-stressed state after a hard day at work. Getting a haircut and dressing in a smart suit might be how one person prepares for an effective day in the office, while another might focus their time on doing their make-up so they look their best, and feel their best, during the day ahead. By aligning our feelings in that moment with a boost to our identity, we engage with our power to be a better version of ourselves, right now.

Making oneself feel good by making oneself look good has long been recognised as an effective state changer. In fact, this technique is so powerful that the Red Cross employed it when they sent relief parcels for the liberated prisoners of the German concentration camps at the end of World War II. Liberating forces were shocked at the scenes that met them when they arrived at the Bergen Belsen horror camp, where the survivors were so emaciated they were barely more than walking skeletons. Bodies were piled up everywhere, people were eating worms because there was nothing else to sustain them, and prisoners were dying in their hundreds before any food or medicine arrived. When aid parcels finally made it to the camp, the soldiers were surprised to find that among the food and medicine was a consignment of lipstick. Yet the effect of such an item was profound.

Lieutenant Colonel Mervin Gonin DSO, one of the soldiers, wrote in his diary:

"This was not at all what we men wanted, we were screaming for hundreds and thousands of other things and I don't know who asked for lipstick. I wish so much that I could discover who did it, it was the action of genius, sheer unadulterated brilliance. I believe nothing did more for these internees than the lipstick. Women lay in bed with no sheets and no nightie, but with scarlet red lips, you saw them wandering about with nothing but a blanket over their shoulders, but with scarlet red lips. I saw a woman dead on the post mortem table and clutched in her hand was a piece of lipstick. At last someone had done something to make them individuals again, they were someone, no longer merely the number tattooed on the arm. At last they could take an interest in their appearance. That lipstick gave them back their humanity."

There are a thousand ways to change your state. If you need to get your intellectual muscles working you can develop writing exercises that will get you thinking. If you want to start the day in a good mood, you can try a positivity journal, as we discussed earlier in the book. But almost as important as things that will improve your mood, energy and state is understanding the things that can harm it.

Ever find yourself drowsy and ineffective after a big lunch? How about feeling sluggish after a late night? Ever notice how wired, sketchy and anxious you can become when you're over-caffeinated?

By understanding ourselves, our bodies, and the things that affect us for better or worse, we can manage ourselves so that we're at our best when we need to be. Alcohol is widely known to be a depressant, and particularly the day after a heavy session it can have a lot of negative side effects. As well as feeling nauseous and suffering from a terrible headache, the psychological effects of a binge can last for days. You don't get quality sleep when you're drunk, it can cause you to become anxious, paranoid, and makes it generally harder to face the day and get stuff done. They don't call the emotional feeling associated with the day after the night before 'the fear' for nothing.

Add the physical side effects of alcohol and you're starting to get quite a recipe for ineffectiveness and negativity. Too much alcohol can cause bloating, which doesn't help your self-esteem when you look in the mirror, especially if you're already feeling anxious and negative. If you're a regular drinker you're aware of what the sugar in alcoholic drinks can do to your physique, and that's before we get on to the health issues around drinking. It messes up your head, your looks and your insides too.

But imagine the self-esteem to be gained from managing yourself by limiting your drinking. Telling yourself that you feel better today because you had the self-control to know when to stop yesterday can be a very satisfying thing. You did something yesterday that you're thanking yourself for today (more on that later).

And it's not just booze that can be a problem. Everything that we put in our bodies has an impact on our state. If we eat too much bread or pasta at lunchtime we can expect drowsiness and low energy in the afternoon, not to mention that all that carbohydrate consumption can easily be stored as fat if we don't burn it off through exercise. The same is true for sugary snacks and drinks, processed ready meals, and foods full of preservatives and artificial colourings. But if we manage our blood sugar levels throughout the day by grazing on beneficial healthy foods, or by fasting until the difficult decisions of the day have been made, then we can remain alert and effective.

Indeed, studies have shown that we're better able to tackle different tasks at different times of the day. We go through a cycle of peak, trough and then recovery, and it has been suggested that we should do our more difficult analytical work during our peak periods early in the day, and then repetitive and non-engaging work such as admin and emails during our trough period after lunch, and then the recovery period towards the end of the day is great for more creative tasks such as brainstorming. Is there a way that we can structure our day around these different states so that we can ensure that we in the more appropriate mindset for the job at hand?

Watching what we eat, and making sure we drink plenty of water can help keep us sharp, in an optimal state for living, decision making and taking action for more of the time. It can also improve our overall health and state of mind. And all we've done is stop eating all the bad stuff. Imagine how much better we'd be if we started eating all the good stuff. If we incorporated more vegetables into our diet, less meat, less sugar, less salt and fat, and started using only fresh and healthy ingredients our general wellbeing would noticeable improve, as well as our ability to function at a higher level and to 'deal with it'.

What if we learned to cook? Not only would we be using fresh ingredients instead of processed products, but we'd be learning a new skill. Suddenly we're mastering an area of life that's good for us, brings great satisfaction and joy, and boosts our power and ability no-end.

And why stop there? As well as putting good things into our bodies to improve our state, what if we were to start doing regular exercise as well, just like the TV presenter I photographed? The physical health benefits of exercise are universally recognised, as are the psychological benefits. But doing exercise doesn't just release happy hormones into the bloodstream that improve our mental health and wellbeing, it's also an extremely meditative activity. Additionally, recent studies have shown that exercise also promotes neurogenesis – the production of brain cells.

Researchers from the Department of Psychology and the Department of Biology and Physical Activity at the University of Jyväskylä in Finland found that consistent aerobic exercise, such as running, promoted the production of cells within the brain. And that's only part of the story. They also found that those people with more brain cells were generally more positive in their outlook and, furthermore, being positive in outlook actually promotes the production of even more brain cells.

So, doing exercise not only makes you happy, but it makes you smarter too. And that, in itself, makes you happier, and smarter. What excuse have you got for not putting on your running shoes right now?

The evidence is irrefutable – eating properly, staying off alcohol, keeping hydrated and getting plenty of exercise gives you a head start when it comes to being in the best state to be effective more of the time. But there's one more vital thing that's often overlooked when we consider wellness, and that's the benefit of sleep.

There's a myth that the most effective people don't need sleep to get stuff done. Indeed "burning the midnight oil" has long been considered a sign of dedication to one's goal. But wouldn't it show more dedication if we were to prioritise being well rested and therefore more capable of giving the important things our full attention. The ideas that "sleep is for wimps", that you can "sleep when you're dead" and that super-achievers can get by with just a few hours of sleep is nonsense. Even British Prime Minister, Margaret Thatcher, who was famously thought to only get five hours of sleep each night was known to take naps throughout the day.

Lack of sleep is now considered to be bad not just for our performance but also for mental health. Tiredness slows down our cognitive processes, reduces alertness and our ability to concentrate. If you don't get enough sleep you're not only more likely to be less effective in that business meeting, but you're also more likely to crash your car on your way to it.

Lack of sleep reduces our learning abilities, so any idea we had of improving ourselves goes out the window, as does any chance of mastering our emotional reactions to situations, as tiredness can be detrimental to mood and our ability to choose the correct behaviour for any situation. And it can lessen our ability to cope with stress, increase anxiety and depression, and have knock-on effects in other areas of life such as healthy eating, exercise and general wellbeing.

We've all experienced that feeling of uselessness and frustration after a bad night's sleep, so why not factor sleep into your wellness regime? Being well rested, fit and healthy, properly hydrated and nourished will enable you to be on top of your game and if you need to change your state at a moment's notice you'll be much better equipped to do so.

CHAPTER RECAP

By recognising the times when we are at our most effective, and using techniques to put ourselves into that state, we can operate at peak performance whenever we need to be. Often state change requires a physical action to initiate it.

Being in the best state to tackle life isn't just about one-off practices and techniques, it's also about being healthy, fit, nourished and rested. Developing a routine that factors all these things is key to developing an effective, balanced approach to life, and to being effective and productive in what we do.

CHAPTER 20: WHO SAYS YOU CAN'T?

"Dream and give yourself permission to envision a you that you choose to be." – Joy Page

I am the youngest child by a long way. My next sibling is six years older than me, and I was always referred to as "the baby of the family". As I grew up, whenever it came to decision making I was always too young to be involved in something so complicated and it was left to the adults. But the problem with being the baby of the family is that you'll always be the baby of the family. Even when I was well into my twenties I was still the baby of the family, and so decision making was always left to the adults, because life is far too complicated for the baby of the family.

I grew up thinking that life is far more complicated than it really is, and assumed that decision making should be left to other people because, you know, what if it goes wrong? I'm the baby of the family, I'm not able to deal with complex issues so I'll leave that to people more grown up, more qualified and capable. Someone else.

Anyone else.

At school, I failed exams because I missed the easy answers while I was looking for the complicated ones. I messed up simple tasks because I was looking for complexities that didn't exist. I stayed away from the frightening realities of finance, of mortgages, of contracts, indeed of any decision making, because I thought it was far too complicated for me, and should be left to other people. To grown-ups.

I put everyone else in the world on a pedestal because they understood all these complicated, grown-up things, were equipped to deal with them and make decisions, while I wasn't, and should really leave that kind of thing to others. I gravitated towards strong people who weren't afraid of the complicated world of decision-making, and in doing so reinforced my status as someone who left that sort of thing to the adults, further sentencing myself to a life of being the baby of the family.

But here's the thing. Nothing is really that complicated.

It was ordinary men and women who sent a man to the moon. Ordinary men and women buy houses every day. Ordinary men and women become brain surgeons. Ordinary men and women lead immensely successful lives. Ordinary men and women have all the things they ever dreamed of, push humanity into the future, and make a reality of complex ideas and notions.

But ordinary men and women also live unfulfilled lives because of bad programming. Just like me, the baby of the family, they think that a life free of hardship and pain is for other people, people who understand the secrets of life, the secrets that they were never privy to. People who are emotionally equipped to make the decisions that they cannot. People they put up on pedestals as an almost superior species of human,

198

completely different to them. People who, in reality, are just like them, but simply have a different perspective.

By the time I reached my early forties I realised that I had never, in my entire life, made a significant decision by myself, without permission or approval from someone else. Indeed, I found myself unable to make decisions – I was always asking what other people wanted, everything was prefaced with "do you mind if...?" and "what do you think about this?" I was totally disempowered, felt like my sense of identity was slowly evaporating, and was so unable to assert myself that I was constantly overridden, was constantly acquiescing, and no longer even knew what I wanted out of life.

I never did anything for myself, simply went along with what other people were doing. Even when it came down to what to have for dinner, or what to watch on television, it was easier to submit to the will of others than to fight for something I wasn't really too bothered about. As a result, I didn't want anything. Worse than this, I burdened everyone else with the responsibility of making all the decisions as I felt I was unable to. I was a drain to be around.

I never bought myself anything, I never made significant life decisions, or even small daily decisions. I was disempowered, unable to take action to better my circumstances. Doomed to be doing underpaid, unfulfilling jobs for the rest of my life, my potential unrealised.

This revelation was a fundamental turning point for me, and it became clear what I needed to do to change things. I set about taking the following steps:

1. In every decision-making opportunity, I needed to take a position. Even if it was something I couldn't care less about, like what to watch on television. It didn't need to be an opposing position to anyone else, but it had to be a solid position.

2. I had to assert that position. Not necessarily a fight to the death, and it wouldn't always require me to get my way, but I had to at least stand behind my choice.

3. I needed to start making decisions, without the approval or permission of anyone else. Decisions that would be beneficial to me.

These three exercises are simple stepping stones to being a more independent, more empowered individual. Being decisive is like a muscle, so by forcing yourself to make even small decisions, you become empowered to make bigger ones, more frequently, and you will find, like I did, that things start to change in your life. You will notice that people will take more of an interest in your opinion, value it more, and see you in a different light. You are no longer the passive voice in the room, waiting to be given direction. You are now an active participant, choosing the direction.

When I took these actions, things started to happen. I started making decisions by myself and for myself. I went out and bought myself a new pair of glasses, replacing the knackered, scratched old pair that I'd been wearing for the last ten years. It made me feel good about myself, and it's important to feel good about yourself, as it helps to reinforce your sense of identity in a positive way as we discovered when we talked about changing your state. A week later, on pay day, rather than put a small amount of my money into my savings account, I invested it instead. Not so much that it would put me at financial risk, but enough that it felt significant. It felt like a decision and I made it myself. I did these things for me and without asking permission from anyone else. And I immediately felt empowered. I was making decisions, and I was doing it all on my own.

The problem is, when we are unable to make decisions for ourselves, when we don't have the strength to do anything other than that which we think others want us to do – our parents, our friends, our bosses, our loved ones, society as a whole – or when we can only do the things that we have permission and approval for, we lose our independence and a sense of our own identity. Our lives are much more likely to go well, whatever that may mean to us, when we follow our own path rather than the path that we think we're supposed to follow. When we do the things that we think other people want us to do, when we select a path to keep others happy, then we are completely and totally disempowered. And this feeds our results. Our lives are not lived with enthusiasm or passion, the path is weak, and the results are substandard or completely non-existent. And we are unhappy.

And what's worse, as our lives are not lived for us, but for others, we lose a sense of what our lives are for, and consequently we lose any real sense of who we are and why we're here. All we know is dissatisfaction, lack of success and lack of independent will, and therefore we assume that these things are a part of our identity. We are so disempowered that we lose touch with all that life could offer us if we could just do things for ourselves, to the extent that we lose any sense of what 'ourselves' even means. We struggle with our identity and our purpose. We have no drive. We find it a wrench to get up in the morning, and we find our very existence a state of constant acquiescence. We start to dread what the day ahead may hold, we yearn for change, anything to make our lives different, even though we've become institutionalised already and are powerless to effect any real change. Life becomes something that happens to us, outside of our influence.

The truth is that we each have huge potential to be extraordinary versions of ourselves, but we dishonour those future versions of ourselves by being unable – or even unwilling – to find the power within us to recognise that potential. And we can only do that when we stop submitting to the perceived wishes of others, and truly look within to find out what we want, what we are capable of, and to take action to realise those things.

We have the power to make change happen, we just need to overcome the resistance to take that first step. We need to create the inertia that will start the motion that will change everything. It doesn't take much, just small improvements, small decisions and small efforts here and there. But soon you'll notice the differences in slight ways, within yourself and in your world. And you will feel empowered to take bigger actions, and bigger still. You'll take failure in your stride as you recognise it as part of the journey to success, and learn from your mistakes to make better, bigger decisions next time. And you'll know that you must never lose momentum but keep ploughing forward, always with a goal in mind.

You've already made a small effort. You've already created the inertia, and you've already started making decisions for yourself. You decided to read this book – at least up to this point – and you did so without anyone's permission.

Do you remember the exercise that I asked you start near the beginning of the book, listing ten positive things each day in a notebook – an exercise I hope you're still doing as part of your daily practice (we'll talk about daily practices later)? Do you remember that I asked you not to mention it to anyone else? That's because the decision to do that exercise was yours and yours alone.

I also mentioned several warnings about that exercise. One of those warnings was that it is really easy to build up a tolerance when carrying out your daily practice, and after doing it day after day, week after week, month after month, you may find that it's not as effective as it was before. That's why it's important to allow your practice to evolve, change and develop over time to keep it varied, to keep it challenging, and to keep it very much personal to you.

So, we're going to add another step to your daily practice, which will help to keep it engaging and effective. You're going to do what I did to make myself a much more decisive person. And after doing it, after having opinions and something to say about things, people started asking for my opinion, valuing it, and taking it into account when making their own decisions.

This is what you're going to do:

1. Develop a want.

   When you find yourself disempowered, unable to have opinions without approval, or without seeking to please others, it is incredibly easy to acquiesce. That is, it's easier to let other people have their way than assert your own will. Over time, you stop having an opinion altogether. But that must change, and this is where you do it. In every and any situation where you might be asked what you want to do, what you think, or what your opinion is, you must ban yourself from saying "I don't mind", or "whatever you think" or anything that excludes yourself from decision making, even though it's a much easier way out. You must force yourself to take a position, and you must express it when asked. That doesn't mean you should argue with people all the time – in fact your position might be in agreement with everyone else – but it is vital that you must force yourself to take a position, no matter how uncomfortable that might feel.

2. Have a reason why.

   So, you've taken a position. Congratulations! Now you need to back it up, otherwise you might as well not have done. It may be that you agree with Jeremy and Susan, in which case say it. It may be that you've seen that movie a thousand times already and you want to try something new. It may be that fish and chips are your favourite because it's important to indulge guilty pleasures from time to time. It may even be that this marketing campaign is targeting the wrong demographic and we should be focusing our attention on the over 60s. Whatever it is, force yourself to have a reason. Your reason may sound stupid, but that's the same risk that everyone who voices their opinion has to face, but this is about being engaged, plugged in, and empowering yourself. And the more engaged you are, the more valuable your opinion becomes.

3. Do something. By yourself.

Every day you need to take action and do something by yourself, without asking anyone's permission, without running it by anyone, and you don't even need to tell anyone about it afterwards either. In an ideal world, it will be something beneficial to you. It could be something that reinforces your sense of identity and makes you feel good about yourself, like getting a haircut or buying a pair of shoes. It could be something small like going for a run around the block. Or it could be something worthwhile like signing up to help at a local charity one afternoon a month. Maybe you want to reach out to an old friend. Or maybe you're going to book the day off work and treat yourself to a lie-in. Give yourself permission to do something, and then do it.

4. Write it down.

    It's time to dig out your nice notebook and pen, because we're going to add to the daily practice. After you've written your daily positive list of ten things that made you feel good, you're going to start writing down the decisions that you've made. This is about celebrating the things that you've done, the choices you've made, and how you've done them yourself, without anyone else's approval, and not to make anyone else happy (unless that was a decision that you consciously made, which is absolutely fine – it's nice to do things for other people). And remember to write about it in the most positive language possible.

5. Do it every day.

    Just like positivity, decision making is a muscle, and the more you force yourself to take a position – even if you couldn't care less – the more you'll be able to make a decision when it really counts, when it really stands for something. You'll start to respect yourself, others will respect your opinion, and you'll become much more dynamic and engaged with life.

When we were children, we left the decision making to the adults. It's easy to still defer decision making to the grown-ups or others that we put on a pedestal because we perceive them to be more capable, more serious, clever or just more adult. But we've forgotten that we are adults. We can make decisions, and take action, and we should, lest we live the lives we assume others want us to live, which is no life at all.

When we leave the decision making to others, we put them on a pedestal and we've already discussed how damaging that can be, as it drains our power. We assume they know better, that they are more capable, better equipped and know more than us. When they confront us we don't question the legitimacy of their action but instead search for an answer that will satisfy them. We feel obliged to do as they say, when really, we should be challenging their authority because, after all, we are adults, just like them. And more importantly, we are at the centre of our Universe, and only we have authority over ourselves.

When someone puts you on the spot and challenges you, do you first look for an answer to their question, or do you instead stop to decide whether to answer? Do they deserve an answer? Are they in a position to challenge you? In the past would you have automatically granted everyone superiority over you? Everyone has the right to ask you a question, but that doesn't automatically mean they deserve an answer.

And when we hold on to our power through independent will and independent decision making, when we take our actions off autopilot and develop a process for being deliberate in everything we do, we have the potential to take ownership of every facet of our existence and in doing so we feel empowered. Strong. Unwavering in the face of adversity. Unintimidated in any situation.

When we introduce an interruption or gap into our old, disempowered process, such as taking time between input and output to breathe deeply, or to adjust our posture, we regain control from our undermining insecurities. We may decide that the correct response was the one that we would have chosen in the first place, or we may decide something completely different. But in that pause, that gap, we create room to make a decision. Our decision.

When we realise the power of consciously responding instead of automatically reacting, of being measured and decisive in every action that we take, from the smallest to the biggest, then we can own our life, we can steer it in the direction of our choosing, and we can choose success and positivity and contentment. So, make a decision right now, that you are not only going to 'deal with it', but you're going to start taking the actions required to live a better life, to move towards the best life, and to start being a better you by moving towards the very best you.

CHAPTER RECAP

You are an adult, and as an adult you are equipped for making decisions. You don't always need the approval or permission of others, and if you arm yourself with the information for making the correct decisions, to create the best outcome, you are as capable of decision making as anyone else. Independent will and decision making are vital for building confidence, overcoming fear and making progress, and for growing your power.

CHAPTER 21: WHO DO YOU WANT TO BE?

"Nothing happens until something moves." – Albert Einstein.

At the end of the first section of this book we stepped aside from our emotional image of ourselves and rewrote our résumé to uncover our superpowers. We listed all the positive things about ourselves, our achievements, positive attributes, skills, traits and abilities that make us shine. We saw that when we remove all the negative self-talk, all the anxiety and insecurity, we have a lot to offer, and that when we choose to look at ourselves in a more positive way, we actually have superpowers.

Now we're going to take that a step further and look forward to the future life that we want to lead, the future person we want to be, and all the things that we need to do to make that a reality. When we know where we want to go we can start taking steps to get there.

Let's undertake an exercise to create a vision of our perfect selves and our perfect lives. First, we need to use our imagination. This shouldn't be hard considering how much we've been using our brains so far in the book, and now we're really going to start indulging ourselves. Let's picture our perfect lives – the lives we're dreaming of. The lives we're already moving towards with tiny steps, steps that are going to get bigger, faster, the more we focus on improving ourselves.

Picture the life you want, but don't focus on the stuff or the money that you have in that perfect life. This isn't about stuff, or material possessions, but about being the version of you that has this life. And it's vital to realise that this is your ideal life, the life you want to live. Not the life of a rock star or a movie star or someone else. This is the life you are dreaming of. You.

Think about what it feels like. Is it a life of financial security? Is it a life of comfort and luxury? Is it a life of health and fitness? Perhaps it's a life of travel and adventure. Or perhaps it's a life dedicated to helping others. How does it feel? What is it about the way this life feels that makes it appeal to you? What is the emotional connection?

Spend some time picturing it, imagining what it feels like to live this life, the kind of work you do, how you would spend your day? And then picture the version of you that lives this life. What are you like? How did you get to this place? What motivates this version of you? What qualities does this version of you have? How different is this future you from the you of today?

Now find your notebook – the one you wrote your résumé in, the one you've been writing in daily with the positive things you're grateful for – and turn to a fresh page. Grab a pen, you're going to make a list.

This list is going to be a series of one or two words, and these words are going to form your new identity. Picture the you from your dream future – the you at your very best – and start writing down words to describe that person. As with the previous exercises, you need to write this in the most positive language possible. Avoid negative words such as don't, doesn't, won't, can't. Replace them with words like is, does, can. And don't stop until you've totally run out of ideas.

Your list, which describes the best version of yourself, might start to look something like this:

Strong / confident / healthy / happy / kind / unswayed by others / smart / sophisticated / graceful / lives life on purpose / kind / a do-er / proactive / clear voice / compassionate / mature / accomplished / independent / fearless / in charge / an ideas person / inspiring / financially secure / brave / interesting / interested / wise / assertive / content / humble / motivated / driven

Keep writing until you've filled the page, then two pages, keep going and don't stop until you've completely run out of words, until the paper is black with ink. And then take a look at the person you've just described. Imagine how that person behaves, what activities they undertake to be like that, how do they think, how do they feel, how do they go about their daily lives both when they're alone and when they're with others.

Now think about your own life, and the way you think, act and go about your daily routine. How different is your own way of living to the way this person lives? Because these are your personal goals. This is what you're going to work towards from this moment forward.

Not having something to work towards is one of the biggest things that makes it seem like you're treading water rather than swimming with the waves. When you're going through the motions of getting up each morning, going to work (if you're lucky enough to have a job), coming home, having the same dinner you always have, and then going to bed, you're simply living life for the sake of itself.

Having something to look forward to makes the hard work feel worthwhile, and rather than wishing your life away, you're instead moving towards something other than just two days off at the weekend. Why else do people have hobbies, play sports, or have another reason for existing beyond that thing they do for money every day?

Now that you have something to work towards, think about the actions you can take to start moving yourself in that direction – improvements and changes you can make in your own life to make you the dream version of yourself. Perhaps this person is slimmer than you. What small action can you take today that, repeated daily, will make you slimmer? I'm not talking about finding a shortcut and going on a diet, but a lifestyle change that will last forever. How can you change your eating habits, your exercise habits, permanently to become that slimmer person? Perhaps that better version of you is more educated, or better read than you are. Can you find time to start reading some classic literature? Can you do an evening class one night a week?

What extra-curricular activities can you undertake to

move you closer to the best version of yourself, to create the life you want? Can you make time to learn a new skill? Can you start to pay more attention to the way you dress? Can you try to be more engaged in your daily routine? Maybe you can start meditating? Or maybe you can start taking more of an interest in the lives of the people you meet, rather than just waiting for your turn to talk?

For some people that extra-curricular activity may be starting their own business, for others it might be building a train set in the loft, and for others it might be losing weight, getting fit, learning web design, martial arts, or how to cook. All of these things are goals, have a process or journey, and turn someone who is ordinary into someone who is extraordinary. And they all deliver a benefit to the person engaged in reaching the goal – whether that's a sense of accomplishment, the possibility of creating the life of their dreams, the body of their dreams, the development of a new skill, or an indulgence in a craft or art. This benefit is the true ultimate goal, but the process is where the work and the power lie.

Goals are not, however, getting drunk every night after work or watching mind-numbing television every evening for the rest of your life, or escaping into drugs or other activities which ultimately are detrimental to the person doing them. As we've already discussed, every action should be done on purpose, and for 'the thing' to deliver 'the power' the action must result in a positive outcome for the person doing it. Your goals are the positive outcome, the power to be achieved, with the side effect that the process can also deliver benefits as beautiful side effects.

Goals and the process of striving towards them give you a reason to restructure and find efficiencies in other areas of your life in order to meet them. For example, perhaps you want to ride a bicycle across the alps. Well, you'll need to organise your garage to find somewhere to put your new bicycle. And you'll need to reorganise your schedule to fit in time for cycle training.

This doesn't necessarily require you to abandon other areas of your life, as we discussed in the chapter about balance. Instead it just means that you balance your life with grace and skill, and find efficiencies and ways to improve your effectiveness elsewhere to not only work towards your goal, but also to become a master in other areas of your existence.

Not only this, but that daily grind, that treadmill that you've been torturing yourself on for years without getting anywhere, will seem a lot easier to deal with now that you have something else to work towards in your life.

Setting goals delivers a sense of purpose, a sense of identity beyond simply being a cog in the wheel. And it allows the goal setter the opportunity to feel as if they have some control over their life and their ability to bring about positive change in it – so long as they are actually engaged in the process of working towards that goal.

In this way, and in the way of this entire book, the process of reaching the goal becomes as important and beneficial as the goal itself. Indeed, it is perhaps more important than the goal because once you reach your goal, what next? You can either go forwards to a new goal or you can go backwards because, as we have already discussed, there is no such thing as standing still. After all, when you stand still you stagnate, and what is stagnation if not moving backwards?

Indeed, Einstein famously stated that "nothing happens until something moves", so rather than having a fixed goal, how about a goal of constant betterment, constant refinement, constant improvement? A goal that is itself an ongoing process? A goal that never ends but becomes an indulgence of discipline, improvement and the ultimate aim of being the best one can be. Goals like this are at the very heart of the graceful living, and living well. Goals like this ensure that life becomes and remains pleasurable in ever increasing amounts. When we refuse to stand still, but remain focused on new targets, new efforts, further improvement, and further mastery, we increase the satisfaction we gain in our own existence, and our potential to improve the lives of others.

When we move constantly, as Einstein said, something happens. We get out of that rut. We start to take decisions. We take risks. We see results. Our power grows. But when we stop moving, we move backwards. And, just as Einstein said, something happens. The results reflect our stagnation. We end up in back in that rut, and we become disempowered. Our results are negative, and so too are we.

Move forward, make beneficial decisions, have a goal in

217

mind, but focus on the process. When the process becomes as important as the goal itself, your life will reflect this with positive results. Get the balance right, make the beneficial decisions, and your circumstances will improve along with them. And maybe, when you focus on the process, you may just meet your goals.

CHAPTER RECAP

Having a goal is an important way of giving yourself a sense of direction and purpose, and helping you choose which beneficial actions to take. It can be a small goal like a project, a hobby, or a pastime, or it can be something bigger like a career goal, or something personal like a health and fitness goal. Whatever it is, goals prevent you from stagnating, which is one of the biggest ways that we can feel stuck and disempowered.

CHAPTER 22: MASTER THE MUNDANE

"Every day, in every way, I am getting better and better." –
Émile Coué

So far in this book we've put our energy into clearing
our minds of the roadblocks, the excuses, the
insecurities that have stopped us taking the action that
is required to own life, rather than letting life own us.
We've even started taking small actions intended to
change our perspective and our approach to daily life so
that we can reframe our current existence in a more
positive way. We've adjusted our lenses, our filters, so
that we can see the world in a more upbeat light, and
set ourselves small daily challenges in order to interact
with the world in a way more conducive to a content,
happy life. We've set ourselves goals, and then decided
to let them go so that we could fall in love with the
process instead. And we have built faith in ourselves so
that we can get there.

But that's just the beginning. Now we're going to focus
on what's required to be the best we can be — to move
forward, to improve and be better. From this point
onwards we are going to focus on action as a method
not just for maintaining a positive outlook – though by
engaging in constant purposeful action of any kind our
outlook will be much more positive anyway – but for
shaping our existence in any way that we wish.

Action is the thing that can make you wealthy. It can give you the body that you want. It can teach you the skills you need. It can give you results of any kind, as long as it is done with intent, persistence, consistency, and a focus on the process rather than the end goal. Purposeful action is not a shortcut, it is a journey of commitment that can take you anywhere you want. And as we know, small repeated actions lead to big results. But they require patience and persistence. As soon as we start to behave like children in the back seat of the car, continually asking "are we nearly there yet?" then we begin to re-introduce the mental roadblocks that we fought so hard to break through – and must continue to fight – in order to reach our goals.

The beauty of action is that it occupies the mind, even when we choose an action such as relaxing for an evening on the sofa (purposeful downtime done with intent is a vital part of a fulfilled life) and prevents those negative inner voices creeping in and sabotaging all our hard work. If you focus on decision making in everything you do, turn everything you do into an intentional action and build a life lived on purpose, that's when you understand your power to achieve anything, and you understand how everything compounds into either a life you desire, or a life of discontent.

Action works in relation to time, and we've already discussed how we exist in three time periods, but that there are only two relevant periods of time that any of us need to concern ourselves with. Today, and the future.

For us to benefit from action today, we need to take action yesterday. Since that is quite obviously impossible, we need to take action today so that we can benefit from it in the future. Sometimes those benefits can be felt almost immediately, and sometimes those benefits can be felt in ten years' time. But there will come a time when that future is no longer the future, and instead becomes this moment right now, and in that moment we will either thank ourselves for taking that action, or we will curse ourselves for not taking action – or for taking the wrong action – in the past. And as we've learned, we can and should only concern ourselves with today and the future, any energy spent cursing the past is energy wasted.

So, let's put positive energy into action right now that will compound into making the future better. Let's build positive habits of action that help to makes us better versions of ourselves tomorrow. Let's start something today that we will be so pleased we did in a year's time.

Let's take action today, and every day, that we will thank ourselves for tomorrow. And we will start in the smallest way imaginable. By making our bed.

At this point I must come clean with full disclosure. The idea of making your bed as a launchpad for productivity and action isn't mine, but I've stolen it from Tim Ferriss, who claimed to have been told it by a Chinese monk. I've seen other writers talk about this technique too, so it's nothing new, but it is perfect in its simplicity, and encapsulates everything you want from action. It is something so easy to do takes minimal effort, and is an action that success (a made bed) or failure (an unmade bed) is instantly obvious.

But just like not eating a greasy burger, this seemingly meaningless task is also easy not to do. It is easy to wake up, get dressed and leave the house without stopping to make the bed. But by not doing this task we are choosing the same behaviour that led us to the situation we are now trying to get out of. We are allowing life to happen to us. Not making the bed is a metaphor for not being able to 'deal with it'. In essence, choosing not to deal with it.

By making the bed, taking a simple action that requires no energy, we are taking ownership of the day. We are planting our flag in the 24 hours ahead, we are taking action, getting the ball rolling with an action that has a guaranteed success, a guaranteed win. And we set ourselves on the path to much more.

Taking action in itself is a powerful thing. It occupies our hands, gives us a point of focus, and in doing so we say, "I am owning this moment". This is why it is so important to build in to our daily lives – as part of our daily practice – quick easy wins, that start us off in a positive way, that we can later build a bigger structure upon to create the big wins that shape our lives and ourselves. By taking action we become doers, people who get stuff done, rather than people to whom stuff gets done. And by taking action we can shape our reality. And it starts with the easiest win of all. Making the bed.

Here's another exercise. Grab your notebook, because

you're going to make a to-do list of easy wins.

What's great about a to-do list is that ticking things off is such a satisfying action that it makes it easy to motivate yourself to do all the things you've listed. This to-do list is going to be about small things that you can do quickly and easily. Household tasks that take little effort, but make a big difference psychologically.

The first two things you're going to write on your to-do list are as follows:

- Write to-do list
- Make bed

The next thing you're going to add is something that is a bit tedious, but makes a big difference, and that is:

- Do the washing up

There's nothing more miserable than a sink full of dirty dishes, but nothing more satisfying than a clean kitchen, and it's always quicker to do than you think. It also illustrates perfectly Emerson's quote:

"Do the thing, and you will have the power."

Life is full of things that we really don't want to do, such as washing up, ironing, studying for an exam, cleaning a messy room. But what all these things have in common is that they have a secret reward that you can gain power from. That reward is the satisfaction that comes once you've done them. You have done the thing, and now you have the power. You have created a clean kitchen. You've taken ownership of that pile of clothes and put them all away, and that feels good. It's been a long day, and last thing at night you have the satisfaction of returning to a beautifully made bed.

You did that. You made it happen. You are a doer.

So, return to your list. What other small things can you add that are easy to do, but that you can tick off quickly and get the reward of success? Put away the washing? Pair up your socks? Go to work? Things that are so easy to do they almost look after themselves?

Don't make your list too long. Just a handful of easy to accomplish tasks that you can complete today without too much of a challenge. And when you've finished writing your list, you can immediately cross off the first thing on it.

- ~~Write to-do list~~

You're already winning. Now go and make the bed.

By creating a to-do list, and putting easy tasks on it, you're getting in to the practice of taking action, and seeing how much you've achieved. It's always important to have a few easy tasks on your list, even when your action scheduling gets more complex, as we'll see later. If you get through the day and there are things that you've done that weren't on the list, write them down and immediately cross them off and then stand back, look at what you've achieved, and give yourself a slap on the back for being so productive.

This exercise of writing a to-do list and dealing with the everyday isn't just about being a tidy person and making sure you have clean plates to eat from. Have you ever heard the saying "life gets in the way?" Well, life can far too often be about the ordinary stuff, the boring chores, the everyday needs, and before you know it you're on a treadmill of wake up, get dressed, breakfast, go to work, come home, chores, dinner, bed. Repeat.

And if you get bored, then these mediocre things can pile up and drown you. But by mastering the mundane – by proactively tackling your day and showing it who the boss is, you are starting something big. By mastering the mundane you are taking charge of a major aspect of your life. And once you've taken charge of it, you'll be able to manipulate it to do extraordinary things, but we'll get on to that later.

Remember, all the great painters had to learn how to paint, before they could create their masterpieces. All the great pianists had to learn to play the piano before they could become maestros. Even Dizzy Gillespie had to learn to read music before he could become one of the all-time jazz greats.

By mastering the mundane we are learning our art, and once we have achieved that, we can move on to fully embracing the art of living and create our masterpiece.

And it's easier than you think.

Build your to-do list. Master the mundane. Become the king or queen of tackling the ordinary. Because very soon you're going to start becoming extraordinary.

CHAPTER RECAP

Small actions, done consistently over a period of time can build into something huge. By undertaking small actions that enable us to master the mundane, we build space to devote to bigger actions that can lead to huge benefits in our lives. Combined with techniques such as goal setting and to-do lists, we can start to do the things that transform us from ordinary to extraordinary.

CHAPTER 23: DEVELOP YOUR DAILY PRACTICE

"An ounce of practice is worth more than tons of preaching."
– Mahatma Gandhi

Throughout our journey, we've been talking about our 'daily practice'. Barely a chapter has gone by where I've not give you a task to incorporate into your daily practice. So it's about time we gave it a bit more attention, so we can see why it's important, and why it's so powerful.

When you're trying to better yourself, better your situation and take ownership of your life, it doesn't take much to knock you sideways. A bad night's sleep can do it. An unkind word from a loved one or a boss can do it. A hangover can do it. A general feeling of 'meh' can do it. That's all it takes for those negative thoughts in your head to start pushing you around, and start you asking, "what's the point?" and "why bother?" all over again. That's all it takes to lose your mojo.

The best way to defend against this kind of thing is to develop what James Altucher refers to in his book, Choose Yourself, as a "daily practice".

A daily practice is exactly what you think it is – a series of actions that you undertake every day, that keep you on course, motivated, and in the best state possible to keep moving towards your goal. Everyone who has a daily practice has a different version of it, but they should be simple things that act beneficially for you mentally, physically and spiritually. But most of all, it should be your daily practice, one that suits your unique daily requirements of life. Not my daily practice, not anyone else's daily practice. Yours and yours alone.

This book already has lots of ideas for your daily practice, and it might include making the bed, followed by drinking two glasses of water, doing ten press-ups and then writing in your positivity journal. It might be 20 minutes of meditation, followed by reading a chapter from a good book, and then a run around the block. It might include actions and activities that you've already started while reading this book – it might be your to-do list, it might be learning how to breathe so that you respond with intent instead of reacting automatically. It might be a series of actions scattered throughout the day at times when you know you might be prone to negative thought patterns, such as after lunch, before bed, or first thing in the morning.

Whatever it is, it's important that it works for you, it is wholesome and healthy, and addresses those three areas – mental, physical, spiritual. It's about priming yourself to operate in the best way you can, to be effective, to own your life, and to be able to conduct yourself gracefully and with control throughout your day. And most of all it's about keeping those negative thoughts at bay, the ones that have held you back all these years and stopped you recognising – let alone achieving – your potential.

As you develop your daily practice, build it so it fits in

with your life. Build it so that it's not stressful to do and is easy to accomplish, and do it so that you feel strong, empowered and motivated afterwards.

Think of your daily practice as the launchpad for the day's endeavours. It's the thing that puts you in the frame of mind for getting stuff done and owning the day and it includes the techniques that we've already mentioned for priming your state, for looking after yourself and being healthy and mentally strong, and a daily reminder which enables you to say to yourself "I've got this".

Your daily practice could involve five minutes where you review your goals and the actions you're taking to reach them. It could be taking time to look back at your journal and see which of the actions you've been taking have had the most impact in your road to self-improvement. It could be five minutes to look at yourself in the mirror and honestly ask yourself if you're doing enough to move along the road to a better you, or if you're trying to do too much. It could be as simple as looking at your to-do list to see which of your mundane daily tasks you sailed through, and which required more effort, and adjusting your approach accordingly.

The daily practice is as much a part of the process as all those small wins we talked about when we examined how to master the mundane. But now that we've mastered those daily chores and everyday duties, we need to make space for those small but vital daily activities, which are essential for successfully moving forward with the rest of your plans. The daily practice is a stepping stone to the next step of achievement, and it's important that completing it becomes an indulgent habit that gives you a moment to reset, refocus, adjust, and move forward.

Perhaps part of your daily practice could be grinding your own coffee beans to make your coffee. Doing something properly like that can encourage you to do your other daily activities with just as much attention to detail.

Perhaps it could be the way you shave your face in the morning. Your daily yoga routine. The way you make your smoothie for breakfast. Your daily meditation, blog post update, walk to the pond at the end of the garden, walking the dogs, or even feeding the cat. It's a time to stop, pause, remember who you are, what you're doing, and then carry on in the right direction.

It's vital though, that your daily routine covers mind, body and spirit, because it's not just about priming your state, but it's also about small compounding actions that will serve you in the long term. Ten minutes of press ups and sit ups, or yoga, or any kind of movement will pay dividends as the years go by. Taking a moment to hydrate yourself will keep you sharp and alert and slow down the ageing process. Focusing on a challenging book will keep your mind agile. Twenty minutes of meditation will keep you calm and grounded.

Whatever the actions you choose for your daily practice, if you choose them well you will feel ready for anything, whole, indulged and at peace as you go forward with your day, your week and your life. It is a foundation for better living, and it is built for you and by you. It is your unique approach to the day, and it should be a moment of bliss that is yours alone to enjoy.

CHAPTER RECAP

A daily practice is a collection of tasks that keep your mind, body and spirit in the best shape for being effective. They help you maintain a peak state, and can include exercise, meditation, reading, planning and journaling. Whatever form it takes, a daily practice is an effective part of the journey to the life you want.

CHAPTER 24: THANK YOURSELF TOMORROW – BE EXTRAORDINARY

"Start by doing what's necessary; then do what's possible; and suddenly you are doing the impossible."
– Saint Francis of Assisi

We've forgiven ourselves for the past. We're using our new capacity to build to-do lists that conquer our day today. And very soon we'll be building a better tomorrow.

The thing about tomorrow is that it isn't here yet, but it stands on the shoulders of what we do today. We can't take action tomorrow, but we can affect what happens tomorrow by taking complete ownership of today.

Currently we're focusing our energy on dealing with today. We're building a daily practice, and we're dealing with things that require our attention right now. Things that are not important, necessarily, but that make a big difference to our state of mind, that show us the power of action in terms of improving our life today with minimal effort, that give us something else to focus on other than the follies of yesterday, and make us do-ers. Things that are mundane, like the washing up and making the bed, but things which, when mastered, make us feel as if we've mastered our life in the present.

The next piece of the puzzle, the next thing on the road not only to being able 'deal with it' but to becoming extraordinary, is about doing things today that we'll thank ourselves for tomorrow. Actions that free us up in the future to focus on bigger things. Better things. What small things can we do today to reduce stress tomorrow, to enable us to be better versions of ourselves, to give us time to work on new projects, build new opportunities, and begin things that in a year's time we'll be glad we started today?

It could be something as simple as setting our alarm clock five minutes earlier when we go to bed, so that we're not late for work tomorrow. It could be something as small as making a sandwich this evening so that we save a little bit of time and money by not having to buy our lunch tomorrow. It could be something as simple as spending a few minutes before bed figuring out what clothes to wear tomorrow so that we save time and don't stress out trying to find an outfit in the morning, which then makes us late. It might be something as obvious as reading through the report before the meeting, so that you have something to contribute. These things – these life hacks – will get us to work on time, stress-free. They'll save us money and give us time in our lunch break to work on that side project, or read a chapter in that book we've been putting off, or book a long-overdue dental appointment. These things will enable us to tackle our days with grace.

I was living in a bedsit somewhere in the Midlands region of England. I had a sink, a bed and a sofa all in one room. I shared a bathroom and a kitchen with two other people who had similar rooms in the house.

The only difference between their rooms and mine was that mine was a mess. I mean, a real mess. I had to climb over piles of dirty laundry, of newspapers, of old plates and cups with mouldy food on them, just to get to my bed. Once I got to my bed, I would have to move piles of paperwork and clothes on to the floor, so I had room to sit and watch the television for the rest of the evening, rather than actually sitting at my desk and doing the work I should have been doing. I was metaphorically buried under all the mess, disempowered to the point where everything seemed pointless. So, I did nothing.

It felt like failure. Everywhere I looked the mess reminded me that I couldn't 'deal with it'. Each morning I would wake up so late that I wouldn't have time to shower. Instead I would dowse myself in deodorant, and rummage through the piles to find some clothes that didn't smell too bad, and I'd head out to class. I was a failure. And I was miserable. It's a stage every young man goes through at least once in his life, usually when they first leave the comfort of home, and realise there no such thing as the laundry fairy.

I would have sorted out my life if I only knew where to start. But that bedsit, that room where I couldn't see the floor because of the mess, had become a metaphor for my life. It was a mess and I would have cleaned it up if only I knew where to begin. The mess was so bad I couldn't see beyond it. And so I climbed on to my bed and went to sleep. I spent most of my days asleep. It was easier than having to look at the piles of paper, clothes, laundry. It was easier to sleep than face the failure that surrounded me. Even my worst dreams were better than the reality of my inability to 'deal with it'.

And then one day I was looking for a pen and I couldn't find one. I knew I had plenty of pens in that room, but they were buried under the mess. So I picked up a newspaper, and I put it out of the way on top of another newspaper. Then I picked up another newspaper, and put that with the other two. Before long I'd collected up all the newspapers in the room into a single pile. I picked up that pile of newspapers and took it out to the recycling bin.

I had taken action. Just a small action. It didn't matter where I had started, but I had started. And I felt empowered.

I went back up to my room. It still looked like the dictionary definition of 'mess', so I picked up all the mouldy cups and plates, knives and forks, I took them into the kitchen. And I washed them all up.

And the next day I bundled up all my clothes, all the socks and trousers and t-shirts that littered the room. I separated them into dark colours and light colours and did my laundry. It was epic.

Before long I could see the floor. So I vacuumed it. And my messy bedsit wasn't messy anymore. It was clean. It was tidy. I had tackled something that seemed overwhelming, and I had done it using small actions. One after another. And bit by bit I had turned a mountain into a molehill. I had reclaimed my space, and it felt good!

In his book, The 7 Habits of Highly Effective People, Stephen R. Covey wrote about the different types of action that people take, and how we spend most of our time taking action that is urgent and important. This can be things like emergency repairs, firefighting, everyday crises, last minute preparations, running for a train, or fixing a car that has suddenly broken-down.

Many of these things could be avoided with some forward planning, but because we are so busy dealing with these crises we don't give ourselves time for that forward planning. And the result is that other things, more boring everyday things, start to become crises that we have to deal with. Things like what to wear for work today, what to eat for lunch, chores like washing the dishes, washing our clothes, doing last minute food shopping. We already have enough things in our lives that are urgent and important, but when the everyday mundanities of life start to become urgent and important too, we become unable to tackle anything else. We lose sight of our goals and dreams because "life gets in the way," and we find ourselves stressed out and exhausted.

Our capacity is so easily filled with these crises that must be dealt with right now – crises that are stressful, need our immediate attention, and are both urgent and important – that we don't have time to do the things which are important but not urgent.

These things, which are important but not urgent, are

the kind of things that get put off until tomorrow, that get overlooked because you've got more pressing things to do (like that meeting, like fixing a hole where the rain gets in, like trying to find an outfit to wear to work) but are the things which could turn your dreams into a reality, or at least allow you to take ownership of your life tomorrow by planning ahead today. They're the kind of things that you think, why bother? It's too huge a task, so I won't even start. I'll never succeed at something like that. People like me don't achieve things like that. Or even just, "I'll do it later".

These are the kind of actions, big and small, that can take your life from ordinary to extraordinary. Often, they don't require a lot of time or effort, but are small practices that, repeated over time, can have huge results. But they are also the kind of things that are easy to put off because you don't have time. You've got dinner to make. You're late for the train. You've got a crisis to deal with. You've got text messages to reply to. You need to catch up with your favourite television programme. You've got a newspaper to read. Things that are either urgent and important, or neither.

The thing is, though, that by becoming a do-er, a master of the mundane, you can begin to structure your life in a way that frees up capacity to do the small things that are not urgent, but are important. As we practiced when we made our to-do lists, we can master mundane things and get a great sense of achievement in the process. And when we can become the masters of all the things that we need to do today – make dinner, do the washing, household daily chores – we can start to make space so that we've got time to begin new endeavours. If you make enough dinner today to last for two nights, you've hacked yourself some time tomorrow evening to work on your new project.

By mastering the mundane and taking charge of those daily activities that eat up our capacity to take steps toward our goals, we can free time to do the things that, in six months, or a year, or in ten years, will transform us and our situation. Because that day six months from now, or a year from now, or ten years from now, is coming towards us whatever action we take. And we can either choose that day to be the same as today, where we wallow in negativity, still stuck in our rut and wishing we'd started something years ago, or it can be a day where we reap the benefits of an action started right now.

To master the mundane, we must develop practices of action that we will thank ourselves for tomorrow. As the saying goes, "the way you do anything is the way you do everything", so by focusing on those small, seemingly unimportant things right now, we are giving ourselves freedom to create bigger things tomorrow.

I would often find that my morning routine was hampered and made much less efficient because getting my clothes out of the wardrobe became a battle of tangled coat hangers, five shirts coming out with each jumper, and a whole load of unnecessary stress along with it. I don't need that kind of tension first thing in the morning when I've got a train to catch. So I removed all the clothes that I was unlikely to wear at that time of year, stored them neatly in a drawer under the bed, and I turned all the coat hangers around so they faced the same way. Add in the practice of preparing tomorrow's outfit the night before, and suddenly I'd saved myself a couple of minutes and a load of stress tomorrow morning.

It's a seemingly minuscule practice, but what I'd done was something that I thanked myself for tomorrow. And tomorrow I was more powerful, more able to 'deal with it'.

I got into the habit of washing up my dishes as I was preparing dinner, so that after I'd eaten I'd have more time available to work on small projects that could build into something bigger. Like writing a few hundred words of a book, planning a podcast, sending an email to someone who might be beneficial to know in my career.

I created a practice that I thanked myself for tomorrow.

I became an expert at putting things away in their logical, correct place, so that when I needed them next I didn't have to hunt around for them. I saved myself time and stress by developing systems and processes that I would thank myself for tomorrow.

I figured out the things that sabotaged my efforts to be the best version of myself – namely bread, beer and sleep. So, I made an effort to plan my lunches to avoid sandwiches, so that I wouldn't get drowsy in the afternoon, I cut down on my alcohol intake so I didn't waste day after day hungover and anxious, and I realised that sleep could be an effective action in itself with regards to being better able to 'deal with it'.

Actions to improve my state. All things I would thank myself for tomorrow.

By developing practices which meant that I had mastered my routine and was no longer spending all my time getting stressed out by firefighting and dealing with daily crises, but was instead living a life on purpose where every activity was consciously carried out with the intention of delivering a beneficial outcome sometime in the future, I freed up capacity in my life. This capacity would be used for actions that were important but not urgent. Actions like going to the gym. Like creating an artistic body of work. Like writing a chapter in a book. Like putting money into investments and savings. Like servicing my car. Like fixing that hole in the roof before it gets big enough to let the rain pour in.

And there was another side-effect too. My to-do list would get crossed off. All those mundane tasks would get done and done and done, and sometimes a task that would inch me closer to a goal would get done too. And I would feel good about myself. A huge sense of satisfaction filled me from within. I wasn't that person anymore, buried under anxiety, negativity, unhappiness, dirty laundry and old newspapers.

Don't get me wrong, those mental roadblocks did pop up from time to time, and they still do. But I became a person tackling life head on. I wasn't putting things off or procrastinating. I was dealing with it. My self-esteem and confidence were growing and I was ready for the next thing.

You see, it isn't hard to be extraordinary. All you need to be is ordinary, plus a bit extra. That's all it takes. But to be that little bit extra, you need to master the ordinary first. You must take charge of the mundane, do tasks before they become crises, and rather than letting them fill up your time so that you have no room for anything more. You must have power over them, so that you can make space for that little bit extra.

Can you steal a few minutes from a routine daily task to give a few minutes to something much more beneficial? Could you watch ten minutes less television every night? Could you hack some aspect of your life to give you space elsewhere? Can you line up your coat hangers so that you're less stressed in the morning? Can you make a packed lunch every night so that the money you don't spend on sandwiches could be put towards a gym membership to fight the flab? If you were to stop making excuses, how could you really start to tackle all those things you've been putting off?

How can you restructure your life so you're doing fewer everyday things that eat up all your time and cause you unnecessary stress, and more extraordinary things that are important but not urgent? The kind of things that will create a better version of you, and a better version of your life?

I was sat at the depot waiting to start my shift, chatting to one of the other van drivers. We were talking about cars, and I mentioned that when I was a child I'd dreamed of owning a Ferrari.

"My brother's got a Ferrari," he said, and he showed

me a photo of his brother's bright red vintage Ferrari on his phone.

I was amazed. Here was someone whose brother had achieved one of my childhood dreams. I asked him what his brother did for a living, expecting to learn that he was an investment broker, or a hedge fund manager, or a banker.

"He's a scaffolder," came the answer.

What? How can an ordinary person, with an ordinary job, have something extraordinary like that? How could a regular person, a person like you or me, someone who wasn't born into a wealthy household, someone who didn't go to a posh school, have something as beautiful as this vintage sports car, that I had only ever been able to dream about. Someone like me could never have something like that. At least that was what I thought.

"He saved up for it," he said.

And there it was. Evidence, if it were needed, of the power of small, positive actions. Actions so small that they seem meaningless, pointless and hardly worth bothering with. But that Ferrari was proof that you don't need to be special to be extraordinary, to have an extraordinary life, to reach your dreams and goals. You just have to take small actions that, over time, will turn into something bigger.

My colleague's brother knew that a small amount of money put away now and consistently over time, could lead to the realisation of a dream later in life. It's that same thinking that makes someone stick to an exercise regime while the rest of us give up because we're not seeing the results we wish for. It's that same thinking that creates a best-selling novel, plants a beautiful garden, realises any dream you can dream of. It's the same thinking that understands that time will pass and things will change, and we either harness that and get on board, or we sink into our rut and let it send us backwards.

On one occasion I found myself sitting next to one of His Holiness the Dalai Lama's Gyuto monks of Tibet. I was listening intently as he chanted a personal puja for me. A puja is a kind of prayer that is made as an offering of respect to the Universe, to act as a blessing to the person for whom it is being chanted. It was an honour to have one chanted for me by this red and orange-cloaked monk, and I had no idea what the words he was saying in Tibetan meant, but it was calming, melodic and hypnotic. Almost trance-inducing.

Behind him three more monks dressed in red and orange were creating a mandala out of coloured sand, a beautifully intricate circular design that can take weeks to complete. Using paper cones, grains of sand are delicately dropped into place to make the shapes and swirls and lines and patterns of the mandala, which can have a variety of meanings.

Creating a mandala like this, one grain of sand at a time, is painstaking work. It requires patience, calm and a steady hand. One sneeze or cough and the whole thing can blow away. Creating it is an act of meditation. But when it is finally complete, after hours, days and weeks of patient work, the mandala is swept up and destroyed by the monks. Some of the grains are sprinkled on the heads of those who have come to pray as a form of blessing, and the rest are usually thrown into a river. In each grain of sand lies the spirit of the whole mandala, and the act of destroying it represents the unstoppable, continuously moving march of time and change.

Life always moves forward, like a river. You can either jump in and swim, or you can stand there and drown. You can either move upward with positive action, or you can move downward with negative action. And you are always taking action whether you're doing it consciously or not, even when you think you're stuck in a rut, going nowhere. Even when you think nothing is happening, everything is changing – it's either improving, or it's getting worse. But it's always moving. Like the story of the mandala, time and change never stop.

There are always things you can be doing to harness the power of time and change to improve yourself and your daily processes. Those systems, habits and behaviours that you can use every day, which in the short term will reflect a life lived on purpose with grace and elegance, and in the long term will have beneficial results that you'll thank yourself for. Maybe not tomorrow. Maybe not next week. It might be in sixty years when you're still active, when you're wealthy, when you're slim, when you're mentally agile. If you adopt an attitude of constant improvement, constant refinement, constant intentional beneficial action, then life becomes an artful experience of experimentation with joy in every detail. And every day you get better, your life gets better, and you enjoy the satisfaction of knowing that you did that.

So, what are the small improvements and refinements that you can make moment to moment that seem insignificant now, but add to the art of living and build up to something huge? Can you turn your morning coffee practice into an art form of measured and intentional actions? Grinding the beans, brewing fresh coffee in a proper coffee pot, warming the milk?

If you have sugar in your coffee, could you go a day without it? A week without it? Could you cut sugar out of your coffee altogether? If you drink a lot of coffee, could you cut down on your caffeine intake by replacing a few of those cups with tea? If you drink a lot of tea could you replace some of those cups with green tea instead? How would that impact your life?

Are there any other routinely small actions that you take every day, that you probably don't even think about, that you could replace with something more beneficial? Could you take the stairs instead of the escalator? Could you walk to work one day a week? Could you turn down the heating by one degree to make your body work a little harder to stay warm? Could you turn the heating off altogether and wear a jumper instead?

Could you cut down on the portion size of one of your weekly meals? How about one of your daily meals? Could you take the leftovers to work for lunch and put the money you saved into a jar on the windowsill? Could you have a meat-free day every week? How about growing your own vegetables?

One evening, why not turn off the television and do something far more constructive instead – like reading a good book? Could you have one day a week where you go a full 24 hours without your electronic devices and enjoy a digital detox? Could you go a whole day without complaining or making excuses?

Are there areas in your life where you can make the most of dead time, time that could be used much more constructively? Could you listen to an audio language course in the car while you drive to work? Why not take a notebook on the train so that you can jot down business ideas during your commute? Can you move your laptop into the kitchen so that you can reply to all your emails, or write the next chapter of your book, while you're cooking dinner? Could you read a personal development book or listen to a podcast while you take your bath?

I was working in a call centre as a telephone fundraiser. My job was to phone people up and ask them to donate to charity. Every day I would make hundreds of calls, one after another, non-stop, from the time I sat down at my computer in the morning, to the time I got up to leave at the end of the day. The majority of calls went unanswered, and the procedure was to let the phone ring for 24 seconds before hanging up and moving on to the next call.

For the majority of calls I had 24 seconds of dead time where I was just waiting, waiting for someone to pick up the phone, or move on to the next call if no one answered. While I worked at that call centre I wrote the entire outline for this book, 24 seconds at a time, while

I was waiting for people to answer the phone. I found a way to maximise the effectiveness of my time so that I could do two things at once, without either action becoming detrimental to the quality of the other.

What are the small everyday things that you could play around with, experiment with, change, improve and replace? Actions which are effortless to make, but compounded over time can have big impacts? How can you hack your daily routine to include improvements, benefits, and the practice of beneficial behaviour, that will deliver improvements for you and your life?

Get your notebook, and find your to-do list. In addition to all the easy wins that you've been ticking off every day, you're going to add two new tasks. These tasks are going to be small things that will build up to have a big impact.

The first is something that you will thank yourself for tomorrow. It's something that you can do today that will free up capacity tomorrow for something bigger and better. Something that will free up capacity for the first step towards a dream. It might be to make a meal plan for the week, that includes some meals that can be spread across two days. It might be organising your outfits so that you don't need to rush in the morning. It might be to reply to all your emails while you make dinner.

The second task is going to be a first step towards a big goal. With the capacity you've freed up in the last task, you're going to start yourself moving down the road towards a dream. You might decide to go for a run to the end of the road and back. You might decide to read the first chapter of a classic novel. You might decide to Google evening classes at the local college.

With the capacity that you've released, you're going to do something monumental, that will transform your life from the ordinary to the extraordinary. That will transform you from being ordinary to extraordinary.

With that free capacity, you're going to start. It doesn't matter where you start. You're just going to start.

CHAPTER RECAP

By embracing the boring aspects of life and mastering them, we can undertake actions today that will benefit us tomorrow, or next week,
or next year. Small actions that either make room for bigger tasks, or make room for compounding actions that build day after day into something much, much bigger. What can you do today that you'll thank yourself for tomorrow?

CHAPTER 25: SIGNPOSTS LEAD THE WAY

"Your heart knows the way. Run in that direction."
– Jalāl ad-Dīn Muhammad Rūmī

On any exercise plan, it's the muscles that you use the least which require the most attention. Those exercises you find most difficult require the most work, and will deliver the biggest rewards or, in the language of the gym – "GAINS."

The temptation, though, is to go with the exercises that are easiest, the weights that are the most comfortable to lift, the cardio machines which you can use with the least difficulty. But conversely, the easier the exercise, the less benefit there is to doing it.

Life can be the same, offering signposts for improvement, in the form of stress, discomfort, hard choices, and obstacles. All these things promise the biggest rewards, and can even be considered as signposts for which direction to turn, which decisions to make, and the best ways to improve ourselves.

This isn't any kind of new wisdom. Why do you think people talk about getting "out of your comfort zone" so often?

But the beauty of using stresses like these as signposts for bettering ourselves, for learning how to 'deal with it' and for becoming extra-ordinary is that, just like everything else in this book, it is incredibly simple to do.

To enjoy the benefits that come along with stepping outside of your comfort zone, you don't have to take a giant leap, nor do you have to make a titanic effort, just a simple little step. A step into something new, something difficult, something frightening, something challenging. And that step may very well offer some sort of benefit, some sort of reward, in which case your comfort zone – and your world along with it – have just grown. But if you don't like where you find yourself, if you realise it's an endeavour you don't wish to pursue or a direction you don't want to go, you can simply step back inside the warmth of your comfort zone.

By taking the road less travelled, opting for the difficult option, we are choosing to better ourselves, to take a small risk and see what happens. And hopefully the thing that happens will take us further down the road of extraordinary.

I was a professional photographer and the host of a podcast. The format for the show was that I would photograph someone interesting and then interview them afterwards. One day I was interviewing an explorer and adventurer, and I was asking her how she became brave enough to do the things she did, to go so far beyond the limits of ordinary people.

She replied that you don't start off going far beyond your limits. At first you just push them a little bit, and when you get comfortable with that, your limits grow to fit your new boundaries. And then you push your limits a little bit more, and they grow again. Even when you're doing something that most people would imagine was beyond any person's reasonable limits, you're never really too far outside your own.

When Neil Armstrong landed on the moon, he wasn't operating beyond his limits. Too much was at stake for him to be the slightest bit unprepared for any eventuality. Such was the duration, extent and depth of his training, the mental and physical preparation that he'd undertaken, that he'd already explored almost every possible scenario thousands of times in the run up to the real thing.

It was every day in training that he pushed his limits, pushed beyond the cosy boundaries of his comfort zone, so that if the time came he didn't have to do anything he wasn't prepared for. And so, when he was on the final approach to the lunar surface and the planned landing zone turned out to be too rocky for a safe landing, he was forced to manually navigate and search for an alternative spot to put down. It was an emergency situation, and the population of the entire world held its breath as it waited to see if the astronauts would touch down in one piece. When the call came back over the radio that "the Eagle has landed", they had less than 25 seconds' worth of fuel left. Yet the whole time he was operating well within his limits.

Part of being able to 'deal with it' means pushing your limits enough that you the master the everyday elements of life, and they don't become your master. It's about developing systems so that you are on top of the small things, the mundanities, that keep the world turning, while you make space for the big things – the things that lead to greatness.

The only problem is, that the everyday things can seem dull or uninteresting, or even unpleasant to deal with. But as we saw earlier, when we talked about building a to-do list of simple quick wins, if we can make an art of these things, truly master them with a sense of grace and accomplishment, then we become the maestro of the orchestra of life, and we can begin to compose our next great symphony.

Part of becoming that maestro is looking for the signposts that lead the way to the things that we must do, things we may not wish to do, but which are the path to success. We must do the thing, and have the power. And as these signposts are often within ourselves, they can be easy to spot if only we can recognise them for what they are.

Have you ever looked at a sink full of washing up and thought to yourself "I really can't be bothered"? That feeling of resistance is your signpost. Do the thing, and afterwards you will get the satisfaction of having done something you really didn't want to do, and you will feel better for it. You will have the power.

Have you ever thought about doing your taxes – possibly the dullest and most boring activity in the world – and thought to yourself "I'd really rather be doing something, anything, else instead"? That tension, that resistance, is the signpost to do the thing.

Nobody likes to pair up their socks, but when you go to your sock drawer and find them in pairs you feel like a winner. Do your taxes, do the washing up, pair your socks. Find success in those wins. Tick off your to-do list. Feel good.

Push your limits. Master the things within them with grace and artistry. Repeat.

When your limits have grown to include all the mundane, everyday aspects of life, you can push them a little further, and a little further still. Now you've mastered the ordinary, and also a little bit extra. Keep pushing. Keep searching for those signposts. Keeping looking for the tension that tells you which way to go.

I was training for the London Marathon. At the end of the road there was a steep hill. It looked awful, so I would always go around it when I went out running. Every time I passed it I wondered what kind of superhero you would have to be to run up that hill. But the thought of trying filled me with dread. It looked so hard, so painful. No-one could possibly want to run up a hill like that.

One day I was going out for my usual training run, and I decided to go for it. I was going to run up that hill. I set myself one rule – that it didn't matter how slow I went, I just had to keep going until I reached the top. I couldn't stop. I had to keep ploughing forward no matter what. This wasn't about being Superman, this was about pushing my limits, and it didn't matter how ugly the attempt would be.

I got to the foot of the hill and took my first step up it. As I moved forward my breathing got heavier and heavier, my pace got slower and slower. I looked down at the ground so I couldn't see the hill going up and up forever ahead of me. I imagined the ground under my feet was flat, and I just concentrated on taking one step, and then the next step and the next. I thought it would never end.

But eventually the ground began to level out. I had reached the top without stopping. I was a panting, dribbling, sweaty mess. I certainly hadn't breezed up that hill, and in fact probably looked like I'd done ten rounds with Mike Tyson, but I was at the top and the moment I stepped on to flat ground everything else felt like a walk in the park.

When I got to the top of that hill my legs wanted to buckle underneath me. I was staggering around like a drunk person, I had snot coming out of my nose, sweat dripping off me, and I was nearly crying. I thought I was going to puke. I staggered past a man walking his dog, who muttered under his breath "fit bastard". Everything is relative!

I felt awful, but at the same time I felt like an Olympic athlete, like a gold medal winner. I felt like Superman.

Every time I went running after that, I would start by running up that hill. Once I got to the top I felt like I could run forever. I could do anything after that hill. And knowing that, understanding the satisfaction, empowerment and sense of accomplishment that came from getting to the top, made the climb worthwhile, and even enjoyable.

When we master the mundane, the boring, those everyday aspects of life, those things that – sigh – we really can't be bothered to do, we get a hunger for action. When we realise that these things really aren't that unpleasant, aren't that dull, and learn to appreciate the satisfaction that comes from completing them, we get a hunger for more. We look for new challenges, new things that we can do to push ourselves and our limits just that little bit further. And we understand that small things, boring things, and even things we complete badly at first – but we complete them nonetheless – are important steps to greatness.

One penny in a piggy bank is the first step to a fortune. One pair of socks paired up is the first step to mastering life with grace and artistry. One more step up that hill is one more step towards being a superhero. And all these things seem boring, insignificant, difficult or unpleasant. But that's exactly what we should be looking for when we want to know which direction to take next, which route to take to better ourselves, push our boundaries and be the best versions of ourselves that we can be.

John F. Kennedy quoted one of America's founding fathers, William Bradford, when he said, "all great and honourable actions are accompanied with great difficulties, and both must be enterprised and overcome with answerable courage."

He went on to say:

"We choose to go to the moon in this decade and do the other things, not because they are easy, but because they are hard, because that goal will serve to organise and measure the best of our energies and skills, because that challenge is one that we are willing to accept, one we are unwilling to postpone, and one which we intend to win."

Overcome the great difficulties, and you will get rewards. Do the thing you don't want to do, and your life will benefit. Find the tension, the thing that is complicated, difficult, boring or hard. Do the washing up. Pair up those socks. Run up that hill. Fly to the moon. Do the thing. Have the power.

Remember, you're already a superhero.

CHAPTER RECAP

The most effective actions are often the hardest, most difficult, or most boring, but by embracing them we can build huge outcomes. Science, chemistry and maths put mankind on the moon. Stop putting off the boring thing, do it now and reap the benefits. Do your accounts. Go to the gym. The thing that you don't want to do is absolutely the thing you should be doing. That's the signpost to success.

CHAPTER 26: MAKE YOUR WHOLE WEEK

"Planning is bringing the future into the present so that you can do something about it now." – Alan Lakein

We spend so much time focused on the things that need doing right now, but offer no long-term improvements to our lives, that we simply spend our lives dealing with the things that need doing right now. The mundane things, the going to work, the making the dinner, the washing, the ironing, the everyday emergencies that will repeat themselves and take up all your time today, tomorrow and the day after that. These things become traps that stop us from doing the things we've dreamed of, and we become so conditioned by this constant battle of the "everyday", that even small dreams, dreams that if looked at objectively are not actually that difficult to achieve, seem far-fetched and impossible.

How do other people keep fit, have time for the gym, set up those side projects and businesses, learn a musical instrument, a foreign language? How do they fit it in? How do they stay motivated? How do they find the time?

The thing is, these people who seem much more on top of life than us, who are doing the things that we would like to do if only we had more time / more money / more energy / more motivation (delete as applicable)

have taken the decision to prioritise these things in their life. They have mastered the mundane, as we discussed in the last chapter, so that they fit around the other much more important things in their life. Their goals.

When you master the mundane and develop behavioural processes, habits and systems that enable you to get the everyday emergencies such as washing up and going to work out of the way in such a manner as it frees up time later in the week, you can prioritise and do those far-fetched things that seem impossible to begin with, but which compound into something much bigger. Mastery like this enables you to start an exercise plan, go for a run around the block twice a week, start an evening course in pottery – to begin to realise your dream.

In doing so, you have chosen to prioritise something that is not urgent, but is much more important in the long term. It is a compounding action that may seem to have no benefit now, but when you fall in love with the process and find the discipline to maintain it long-term, the rewards you reap will be significant.

Stephen R. Covey talks about the importance of scheduling your priorities instead of prioritizing your schedule, and this a super-powered way of getting things done. You're already good at doing this with the to-do list that you started using when you began mastering the mundane, but now that you're a master, we're going to step things up a notch and do what Covey recommends by turning our to-do list into a week planner. We're going to start really becoming productive, taking charge of our time, and as well as simply getting things done we're going to start the slow but satisfying task of building our futures.

When we talk about building the life of our dreams it's impossible to move towards it unless you know what that dream looks like. So, you need to get a clear vision in your head about the shape and structure of the life you want. Go back to your notebook and start to write about it in the clearest, most positive terms. Use positive phrases – instead of saying "a life free from struggles" describe it as "a life full of comfort", instead of saying "I want to build a business that doesn't fail" phrase it as "a business that succeeds". Use positive terminology, and paint a real positive picture. Rather than simply saying "I want to be a millionaire", describe "a life of abundance". Rather than saying "I want to be less skinny" say to yourself "I want to be fit, strong and in good shape." Let your imagination go, let the pictures flow, and be as positive as possible.

When you have a clear, detailed picture in your head, that's your ultimate goal. Now, are there any sub goals that you can break your ultimate goal down into? If, for example, your ultimate goal is to become a world class swimmer, perhaps a sub goal could be to learn how to swim. If your goal was to learn another language, perhaps your sub goal could be to find an evening course to sign up to. If you want to be a jet setting, globe-trotting entrepreneur, maybe your sub-goal could be to have ten business ideas every day. If your goal is to be a much happier person, maybe your sub-goal would be to go a whole day without complaining.

When you've developed your sub goals, ask yourself if

they're suitably small stepping stones for you to start working at, or whether you need to break them down even further. If, for example, your goal is to be an astronaut, and your sub goal is therefore to be a test pilot, do you need to research flying schools near you? Could you think about buying a beginner's guidebook to aviation? We're looking for small, bite size tasks that seem doable, realistic, but which play a key role in you bigger ultimate goal.

Now that you have a decent understanding of what needs to be done to start you moving along the road to your ultimate goal, we're going to return to your to-do list, and we're going to supercharge it. It's going to become a week planner.

Simply put, a week planner is a to-do list set against time. It's a large piece of paper with the days of the week down one side of it, and then boxes to write in the tasks to be done each day. What's beautiful about a week planner is that you get to see, at a glance, where you spend most of your time during the week, and where you can make space for the activities – or sub goals – which will move you towards your ultimate goal.

The first thing that you're going to write into the boxes are the mundane tasks that need to be done. You're going to schedule your daily emergencies, the chores that need to be done for the wheels of your daily machine to keep turning. This includes the washing up, cooking dinner, the ironing, going to work every day and the things that you must do daily.

The next thing you're going to put into each day is your daily practice. Making the bed, meditation, drinking water. Those little tasks that benefit your mind, body and spirit and lay the foundation for the great things that are to come, and will ultimately help to set up your state so that you can be at peak performance for the day ahead.

Now take a look at your planner and see your week unfolding. How does the piece of paper in front of you relate to your actual week ahead? Can you move any tasks around to free up time so that you can work on your goals? Can you move anything to Tuesday so that you can put time aside on Monday to work on your business plan? Is there anything that you can do on Sunday evening that will impact the rest of your week to reduce stress, create space, and allow you to take ownership of the days ahead? Could you, for example, prepare your lunches for the week, or iron all your shirts so that you can save time each evening and morning for that new project you want to get started on?

And think about your levels of effectiveness. When I was working shifts into the night as a delivery driver, I knew that by Thursday I would start to get extremely tired, so I would start to schedule power naps for when I got home. This would enable me to be better equipped and more alert when it came to working on my goals. I would schedule the bulk of my priorities for Monday and Tuesday, and start to ease back towards the end of the week when I needed to give more attention to my physical, emotional and psychological wellbeing.

This week planner is a chance for you to craft the seven days ahead, to embrace the art of living and to make plans to accomplish things beyond the everyday, things that are extraordinary. Each day as you make the bed, go through your daily practice, go to work, do the washing up, and spend an hour working towards your goals. Cross them off your planner. If, by the end of the week, you have found that some days you've been over ambitious, and you weren't able to cross everything off, then next week keep that in mind as you prepare your plan for the next seven days. This is a constant work-in-progress after all.

If you have one big goal that requires extra work, put aside several days for it, and schedule everything else for another time. Know yourself and what you're capable of, know if you're aiming too high, understand that sometimes unexpected events will occur which mean you will have to abandon your week plan for a while, but have the discipline and enough faith in yourself to return to it when the time is right.

The week planner is part of a treasure map to the goals you seek, and it's also a mirror that reflects you, what your ambitions and dreams are, and what you're really capable of when you put your mind to it.

As the weeks go by, and you develop a mastery of week planning, take it a step further. Set yourself a monthly goal, and see how your week planner can help you reach it. And then try a six-monthly goal, or a year goal.

See how you can use your week planner to develop

practices and actions that will become part of your routine, and it will build into something that you will thank yourself for tomorrow, and in twelve months' time. See how taking ownership of your time, of your daily life, of your decision making makes you feel more capable, more confident and boosts your self-esteem. Understand the power of a life lived gracefully and on purpose, and make every action intentional and beneficial.

CHAPTER RECAP

When we take ownership of our time – our days and weeks – and master the everyday things that need doing so that we can create space in our week for activities that move us towards our goals, we see real progress. Furthermore, we are able to manage ourselves so that we can be most effective in pursuing a gracefully lived, masterfully managed life that not only moves us forwards, but delivers satisfaction and joy in the process.

CHAPTER 27: THE IMPORTANCE OF DISCIPLINE

"With faith, discipline and selfless devotion to duty, there is nothing worthwhile that you cannot achieve."
– Muhammed Ali Jinnah

We've already talked about the importance of doing things that may not bring immediate results, but that we may thank ourselves for later. Sometimes this involves doing the things that you don't want to do now so that you can enjoy the benefits in the future. Every morning we make the choice between staying in the warmth and comfort of our bed, or getting up to face the day, to go to work, to brave the cold floor under our feet when we reluctantly pull ourselves from under our duvet. This is what discipline looks like, and it's the difference between taking the easy option that will deliver a small gratification right now, or the difficult option that will deliver a bigger result later.

Employing a practice that brings a better life, a better version of ourselves, means making the effort right now to do something that might be hard, unpleasant or dull. Finishing that report, ironing those shirts, learning how to write a business plan, going for that six-mile run in the rain, not having that last drink tonight so that we'll feel much better in the morning. It all takes discipline. Discipline towards a bigger goal, a long-term aim or objective.

That discipline is about deciding who you want to be and doing the things necessary to become that person. About choosing confrontation over sitting back, about asserting yourself rather than letting others overrule or undermine you, about making the effort that is required to say to yourself "yes, I can", and taking responsibility for honouring the potential within you.

The problem is that discipline is hard work, and often it is hard work repeated consistently over a period of time – in some cases over a lifetime. And that isn't always immediately appealing.

It would be much easier to have that extra slice of cake and the immediate pleasure that comes with it. It would be much easier to stay indoors and not go to the gym. It would be much easier to switch on the television rather than spend the evening working on that presentation.

But discipline is what separates the achievers from the non-achievers. It's the difference between the person who keeps their job and the person who gets the sack because they didn't turn up. It's the difference between finding out what you're capable of, or remaining cosy and warm inside your comfort zone.

Ultimately, though, discipline is the thing that proves to you that you are someone who can achieve things. Discipline is the thing that builds confidence in your abilities. Discipline says I can run to the end of the road, and tomorrow I'll run further.

And the beautiful thing about discipline is that it

compounds, makes us stronger, and if practised enough it can become pleasurable in itself. There is satisfaction to be found in being able to subjugate your immediate desires, safe in the knowledge that you will receive a greater reward tomorrow. While the people sat on the sofa may criticise you for what you're doing, you know that you're doing something. While the people who have failed to lose weight will try to discourage you, you know that your discipline will enable you to succeed where they did not. While some people think you're daft for starting that side project, discipline tells you that without action there can be no success.

Discipline is about character. It's about saying this is who I am. I am capable, I can succeed, I'm not going to let fear stop me from attempting what others think is impossible. Discipline is about having integrity to follow through on your plans, and to respect and honour yourself and your potential enough to make the effort to be the best version of yourself possible. It's about doing the small things, paying attention to the details, and not putting off until tomorrow those beneficial and positive actions that you should be doing today.

Discipline says I'm not afraid of complicated things, and I will learn to understand them, and I will not be intimidated. I'm going to push myself beyond where I am today, and step up to the level required to do that thing that most people will not. It's about taking the necessary steps to replace those negative behaviours and actions (or inactions) that have become masks behind which we hide our true, best selves. Those masks that have become an excuse for laziness and disempowerment.

When we don't take the time and effort to build a daily practice that takes into account our own wellbeing, our true potential and the things we are striving to achieve, we are dishonouring and disrespecting ourselves and all that we can be. A person without discipline is like King Arthur, had he not made the effort to pull the sword from the stone.

At first discipline seems like difficult work, and at first it is. But the difficult work eases when inertia gives way to momentum, and in that moment actions become effective, dreams become realistic, goals become reachable and processes become rewarding. In that moment, discipline begins to feel like an indulgence of someone who is mastering the art of graceful living.

When I worked as the van driver, I had the discipline to pull myself out of bed at 3.30am on a cold winter morning, to deliver groceries. When I was a carer for the disabled I had the discipline to subjugate my own needs for those who relied on my empathy to bring them dignity throughout their day. When I was a journalist I had the discipline to represent the truth in a way that was compelling and did justice to the story I was telling. As a person I must have the discipline to do justice to my own potential, to the breadth and depth of the world I can build for myself, and to make the most of that which life can offer me.

Life is like a vast playing field, and we are thrust on to it the moment we are born. We can either choose to wait on the side-lines to be called for our turn to play –

which is unlikely to happen – or we can stride on to the pitch and bring our best game. Discipline is the commitment to being the best sportsman, in the best shape, and with as much drive as possible. And when the final whistle blows, we should be able to say we played as best we could.

Discipline is the secret ingredient that brings all the other parts of the recipe together. The positive perspective, the self-confidence, the ability to subjugate our emotions so that we respond rather than react, the state priming, and the process in order that we can move towards our goal. If process is the wheels on the car, discipline is the energy that turns them, and doesn't stop until you get to your destination.

In our own self-management (and that is the territory into which we are now venturing) we must ensure that our processes work for us, but that we have the discipline to be able to step aside from them when a problem or opportunity arises, knowing that we will return to them afterwards. Because problems and opportunities do arise, and no amount of weekly planning can account for that. There are times when you must put the process on hold, deal with whatever emergency or event requires your attention, and then return to the plan later.

We must not be trapped by our processes, but like a grass that bends in the wind without breaking, we must be flexible enough to know when to step off the path we are following, if only for a moment, while still applying our philosophy of being our best selves. All the while our faith in ourselves will be supported by the knowledge that we have the discipline to return. When we know this to be true, and we know the commitment we have to ourselves, then we are unstoppable, adaptive, and able to reach any heights we set our sights on. Our processes are the tools with which we achieve our goals, but they are not our masters. As with any tool, it is only powerful when wielded properly, and we must know which tools to use and when to maximise our effectiveness, in order to better ourselves and the things we do. We must not be slaves to our processes, but we must choose to use them with discipline and flexibility. Similarly, our processes must not be blinkers, they must not become the kind of new filters that stop us seeing the world with empathy and from the perspective of others. We must still be aware of everything around us, the perspectives of others, and we must be objectively aware of our own perspective in that we might correct our course should we find ourselves disappearing into unpleasant territory.

With the tenets of kindness, empathy, action and goals leading us, we can move forward not only improving our own lives, but also the lives of those we encounter – even if it's only a small way. If we can be disciplined in our own character we can leave each person with a gift. It may be a laugh or a smile, it may be that they feel valued or worthwhile, it may be that they've learned something, or even that they've imparted something worthwhile, but with the same discipline that we honour ourselves, we can honour others. And that in turn adds to the grace and artfulness with which we live our lives.

Discipline is integrity in action.

CHAPTER RECAP

When we act with discipline, it reinforces our self-esteem and sense of self-worth and, ultimately, our power. Discipline is the force which puts everything into practice, and keeps it there, building, growing, getting stronger.

We must show discipline if we wish to improve, have a better life or be a better person. And only through discipline can we prove to ourselves, and the Universe, that we have mastered the art of graceful living.

CHAPTER 28: THE DIFFERENCE BETWEEN HARD AND DIFFICULT

"It is not because things are difficult that we do not dare, it is because we do not dare that things are difficult."
– Seneca the Younger

When you've been watching life go by every day wondering when it's going to be your turn, waiting for the time when you're going to be called to pull the sword from the stone and find your inner King Arthur, you've been missing the point the entire time. When you feel like you've been working really hard at life and you're not sure why you don't yet have your reward, it's because you've failed to recognise the difference between hard work and difficult work.

For over a year I woke up at 3.30am, drove through the night to carry roughly a tonne of groceries up to the front doors of customers who didn't know that my legs ached, my hands were torn to shreds and my arms constantly ached. They didn't know that I had rarely seen my wife for more 30 minutes a day for over a year, just so that they didn't have to go to the shops.

For three years I cleaned up urine and faeces for the minimum wage. For two years I was bullied by a sociopathic boss. I worked jobs where I had to care so much my heart was broken daily because I was forced to work within a system that didn't look after the people it claimed to support. I spent years dragging heavy photographic equipment through city streets to clients who paid me pennies but still thought I was too expensive. For years I was unhappy because no matter how hard I worked I never got my turn, and I never had anything but self-doubt and insecurity to show for it.

The work I did was hard, but it wasn't difficult. I never did the difficult thing and pulled the sword from the stone. I thought that was for people cleverer than me, stronger than me, who were more gifted than me. But those gifts, those things that other people had which I didn't, they aren't gifts at all. They aren't things that are given to people. Those gifts are something you give to yourself through dedication, discipline, and by doing the difficult thing. And, of course, by giving yourself permission, approval and validation.

The gifted swimmer got their gift through years of practice, of working towards a goal, of having faith in themselves and their efforts. The gifted businessperson got their gift through years of reading the books, doing the exams, and subjecting themselves to real world experiences. The gifted artists got their gift by toiling towards a dream. The gifted overnight sensation got their gift by spending decades honing their craft, practicing, and moving towards that one night where they would be revealed to the world. These things are difficult, and they can also be hard. But some things are just hard.

Hard work rewards you with a paycheque at the end of the month, if you're lucky. It may reward you with a gradual automatic progress up the career ladder. It may give you everything you need to make ends meet. But often it does not.

Difficult work requires difficult decisions. It requires the discipline to do things that you don't want to do but leads to something bigger. Difficult work requires you to put your insecurities to one side in order to take the risk, make the decision, voice an opinion, choose between one option or another, or to suggest an entirely new option altogether. Difficult work tells you to turn off the television in the evening and to spend that time doing your coursework, making that business plan, doing the paperwork, learning about subjects that bore you so that you can grow and develop. Difficult work is doing the thing, so that you can have the power.

Meanwhile hard work keeps you down in the mine shaft chipping away at the coal face. It keeps you stacking shelves, breaking your back, wondering when you'll get your slice of the pie. Hard work just about keeps the wolves from the door – if you're lucky. Hard work is the work done by those who are a cog in the machine, rather than those who are building the machine.

Don't get me wrong, hard work keeps the world turning. There are people who came before us and who will come after us who worked hard their whole lives, whose sweat, blood and tears have built the tallest skyscrapers, the cargo ships that keep the global economy going, and the empires that spanned the planet. And don't misunderstand me – difficult work is also hard. But difficult work moves you forward, it improves you, improves your situation, and takes you closer to your goals. It's not going to be easy, but the rewards will be much, much greater.

Think about this: Isambard Kingdom Brunel is remembered as one of the men who drove the industrial revolution. He is remembered as the man who built dockyards, tunnels, bridges and railways. He drew the designs, created the plans, devised the processes that became the infrastructure upon which modern society is built. Difficult work. Hard work.

But who remembers the brick layer who built the vast supports that hold up his bridge at Clifton in Bristol? Who remembers the steel worker who installed the furnace in his mighty steam ship The Great Britain? Who remembers the rail worker who laid the tracks for the Great Western Railway? Who remembers the six workers who drowned when the roof of his tunnel under the River Thames in London collapsed?

All these people, whose physical exertion, whose torn muscles and broken bones lay testament to the power of hard work, broke themselves in order to put a roof over their heads, to feed their families. They worked hard for someone else's dream. That is hard work.

So the question is this: Are you going to do the hard work to realise someone else's dream, or the difficult work to realise your own? Are you going to be the version of yourself who does the difficult job of pulling the sword from the stone, or are you going to do the hard job of doing what you've always done, hoping for a reward that will never come? Will you keep getting by, taking comfort in your rut and the misery of forgotten dreams, or will you start taking the small steps to freedom, to making decisions that boost your confidence and benefit you in other ways?

Are you prepared to do the difficult work it takes to become King Arthur?

I've lived a thousand lives, been a thousand different people, in a thousand different places, and all along there was only one place I wanted to be. But the harder I tried, the further away it seemed to get. That place I wanted to be, the thing I desired the most, was success.

We've all lived a thousand lives, from one day to the next, and success is with us always, just like our power. But often we carry it out of sight, like a burning ember waiting to be reignited into a roaring inferno by positive action.

And it is positive action that will grow our power and our success. When we embrace joy, embrace positivity, embrace forward motion, and embrace the small steps that we can take every day to build something bigger, we will grow our power and find success. When we engage with life, with positive action and a positive attitude, then life will be ours and so will our power and success.

All we have to do is refuse to be afraid of any task, situation or person we may face, and with that fearlessness embrace change and transformation. Transformation of perspective, of thought, of emotional reaction, and of action. And by doing so we will witness a transformation of results.

It will be hard, but not as hard as you think. It will take a long time, but not as long as you think. And once you start to see the results, you will get a hunger for improving a little bit more, every day. A hunger for taking only action that is beneficial. A hunger for living life on purpose.

You've come this far. You've already started. Don't stop now. This is just the beginning.

ACKNOWLEDGEMENTS

Throughout my many lives I've met a lot of amazing people. Some have encouraged me to start something, some have had a profound impact on me, and some have been there offering support, reassurance and wisdom. Others have inspired me in person or from afar, while others have held my hand as I've stumbled along trying to find my way. Others have kept me sane and others just have a special place in my heart.

Whatever their role, all these people have been fundamental in getting me to this place, here, right now. This is where I acknowledge just a few of them – in truth there are too many to list and this just scratches the surface. But if you're not on this page, know that you're in my heart. So, in no particular order:

Iro Ouranou, James Altucher, Bob Proctor, Carlton Coulter, Everton Bell-Chambers, Miroslav Jesensky, Jake Hughes, Jenny Crompton, Bowa, John Greenhalf, Shea Lewis, Michelle Butler, Chrissa Amuah, David Cronenberg, Sue Stone, Jeff Olson, Tim Ferriss, Stephen R. Covey, Seth Godin, Naval Ravikant, Kerry Clancy, Jaki Windmill, Dr. Shakeel Bhatti, Sven Goewie, Mathie Neven, Dave Read, Inge Tranter, Jakob Stig-Nielsen, Kristoff Bertram, Michael Richardt, the Gyuto Monks…

… and all the countless people who have influenced me, guided me, made me think, and made me care throughout my life.

ABOUT THE AUTHOR

Chris Brock is a multi-award winning creative living in the countryside somewhere in the South of England. He has worked with organisations such as Microsoft, Ford, Johnson & Johnson, the BBC, Singapore Airlines and the Discovery Channel, and his work has appeared in publications such as Vogue magazine, Cosmopolitan, The Guardian and The Daily Telegraph.

He has also worked as a carer for the disabled, and a van driver, and an emergency telephone operator, and a warehouse operative, and a charity fundraiser, and a facilities manager, and a shop assistant, and a kitchen hand, and a market trader, and a magazine editor in London and New York. He's handed out flyers on street corners, sold stereos on the high street, spent two days working as a mortgage advisor, and even appeared in a sitcom. As himself.

You can find more of his writing at www.chrisbrock.uk.

27509777R00167

Printed in Poland
by Amazon Fulfillment
Poland Sp. z o.o., Wrocław